¡Búscalo!

DATE DUE

NO ✗ 1 ℔			

PRINTED

R

¡Búscalo!

(Look It Up!)

A QUICK REFERENCE GUIDE TO SPANISH GRAMMAR AND USAGE

William M. Clarkson, Ph.D.
Guillermo Campos

John Wiley & Sons, Inc.

New York • Chichester • Weinheim • Brisbane • Singapore • Toronto

This book is printed on acid-free paper. ∞

Published by John Wiley & Sons, Inc.
Published simultaneously in Canada.

This publication is designed to provide accurate and authoritative information in regard to the
subject matter covered. It is sold with the understanding that the publisher is not engaged in ren-
dering legal, accounting, or other professional services. If legal advice or other expert assistance
is required, the services of a competent professional person should be sought.

Library of Congress Cataloging-in-Publication Data

Clarkson, William M.
   ¡Búscalo! = Look it up! : A quick reference guide to Spanish
grammar and usage / William M. Clarkson, Guillermo Campos.
      p.   cm.
   ISBN 0-471-24560-7 (pbk. : alk. paper)
      1. Spanish language—Grammar—Handbooks, manuals, etc.
I. Campos, Guillermo.   II. Title.
PC4112.C53   1998
468.2'421—dc21   97-40782

Printed in the United States of America.

10 9 8 7 6 5 4 3 2 1

Introduction

Whether you're a serious student of Spanish or just a curious learner of the tongue of Cervantes, *¡Búscalo!* can help unravel the sometimes baffling peculiarities of Spanish grammar and usage. *¡Búscalo!* is not a textbook with little gems of wisdom tucked away in some supposedly strategic sequence of chapters. *¡Búscalo!* is a user-friendly guide and reference tool designed specifically to provide quick, concise, and reliable answers to common problems that confront the language learner.

For any student of Spanish, finding a quick answer to a grammar or usage problem is not always easy. Although traditional Spanish textbooks have their indexes, these may not provide a ready solution to the problem at hand; in fact, the search may prove more vexing than rewarding. The textbook may have the desired material, but it may be difficult to retrieve, or it may be scattered throughout the text. For example, how does one express the English word *may* in Spanish? The typical textbook does not have an entry under *may* in its index. What are the uses of **lo?** If there happens to be an entry for **lo,** it likely directs the student only to "direct object pronouns" and omits references to its other uses, for example, as a neuter article.

What makes the material of *¡Búscalo!* so accessible is that all entries are in alphabetical order and in many cases are cross-indexed. If the reader wants to know how to express *may,* a complete discussion can be found under the heading MAY (p. 113). And for a complete treatment of **lo,** see LO (p. 109). It is not necessary to chase down incomplete cross-references and then consult several chapters to obtain an understanding of the meaning and usage of these words.

Troublesome or confusing words find ready solution in *¡Búscalo!*. For example, the possible confusion of **pedir** *(to ask for)* and **preguntar** *(to ask)* is unraveled under the entry ASK: PEDIR *VS.* PREGUNTAR (p. 28) with cross-references under the individual entries of PEDIR and PREGUNTAR.

¡Búscalo! is not only handy but comprehensive as well. **Ello,** a pronoun meaning *it,* goes unrecorded in most Spanish textbooks but receives thorough treatment in *¡Búscalo!*. The explanations are brief, and the examples are clear. So for students of Spanish who want a quick answer to a language problem, they can **buscarlo**—*look it up*—and find it in *¡Búscalo!*.

A Note on Pronunciation

In general, letters of the Spanish alphabet, particularly the vowels, represent fewer sounds than letters of the English alphabet. The following descriptions of the sounds of Spanish vowels and consonants are approximations.

VOWELS

Each Spanish vowel represents (phonemically) one sound that is shorter, sharper, and without the glide that often accompanies English vowels. For example, the word *no* is the same in both languages, but the Spanish **no** is short and crisp and does not have the offglide [\w\] of the English *no.*

A

The Spanish **a** is pronounced like the *a* in the English interjections *aha!* and *ha-ha!:* **casa, lana, pata, mata, lata.**

E

The Spanish **e** is pronounced like the *e* in the English words *met* and *set:* **me, de, Pepe, le, te.**

I

The Spanish **i** is pronounced like the *i* in the English words *piano* and *liter:* **mi, ti, si, mil.**

O

The Spanish **o** is pronounced like the *o* in the English words *go* and *so,* but without the glide: **los, polo, lodo, oso, toco.**

U

The Spanish u is pronounced like the *u* in the English words *rude* and *dude:* l*u*to, m*u*la, ch*u*la, p*u*so, p*u*ma.

When followed by a vowel, it sounds like the English *w:* b*u*eno, g*u*ante.

The u is always silent after q: *que, qui*nce. It is also silent in gue and gui combinations: *gue*rra, *gui*tarra. However, it is pronounced in these two combinations when written with a dieresis (¨): pin*gü*ino, a*gü*ero.

CONSONANTS

The following Spanish consonants represent essentially the same sounds in both languages: f, k, m, n, p, s, t, w, y.

B

b at the beginning of a word or following an m is like the English *b* but less plosive (the lips are not pressed as tightly together): *b*ota, am*b*os. In all other positions it is softer, with the lips barely touching: tu*b*o, ta*b*la.

C

c before e and i is pronounced like English *s: c*inco, *c*elos. In Spain, c before e and i is pronounced like English *th* in *th*ick. In all other positions it is pronounced like *k: c*una, a*c*to.

CH

Spanish ch is always pronounced like *ch* in *ch*urch. As a result of changes made by the Spanish Royal Academy in 1994, ch is no longer considered a separate letter for the purpose of determining alphabetical order.

D

d at the end of a word or between two vowels is pronounced like the English *th* in the word *there:* to*d*o, dormi*d*o. In all other positions it is closer to the English *d* in the word *dollar* but still with a hint of the *th* sound of the word *then* because the tip of the tongue touches the edge of the front teeth.

G

g before e and i is pronounced like a strongly aspirated (harsh) English *h: g*eneral, *g*itano. In all other instances g is pronounced similar to the *g* in *got:* *g*ato, *g*ota, *g*usto, in*g*rato.

H

h is always silent: a*h*ora, *h*abla.

J

j is pronounced like a strongly aspirated English *h* (the same as Spanish **g** before **e** or **i**): *j*inete, *j*oven.

L

l is similar to English *l,* but the tip of the tongue lies at the base of the upper front teeth and does not curve up toward the palate as in English: *l*ejos, *l*odo.

LL

ll is usually pronounced like the *y* in *yellow:* ca*ll*e, pasti*ll*a. In Spain, **ll** is pronounced like the *lli* in the word *million.* As a result of changes made by the Spanish Royal Academy in 1994, **ll** is no longer considered a separate letter for the purpose of determining alphabetical order.

Ñ

ñ is pronounced like the *ny* in the English word *canyon:* a*ñ*o, le*ñ*a, pi*ñ*a.

Q

q only appears in the combinations **que** and **qui,** and the **u** is silent in both cases: a*qu*í, po*qui*to, por*que*, *que*so.

R

r within words is usually pronounced with a single trill or flap of the tongue: pe*r*o, ca*r*o, pa*r*a.
At the beginning of words or after **n, l,** or **s,** the trill is extended: *r*ápido, En*r*ique, al*r*ededor, Is*r*ael.

RR

rr is pronounced with the extended trill and is never written at the beginning of a word: pe*rr*o, ca*rr*o.

S

Spanish **s** is similar to English *s,* but it is never voiced (\z\) between vowels as it sometimes is in English (*rose, president*): ro**s**a, pre**s**idente.

V

v is pronounced the same as Spanish **b** and not like the *v* in *very:* *v*a, *v*iernes, moti*v*o.

X

x is usually pronounced like an *s* or *ks* before a consonant (**explicar**), like *gs* before a vowel (**exigir**), and in certain words of Mexican derivation, like an *h* (**Texas, México**).

Y

y is pronounced like *y* in *yes:* **playa, maya.** y meaning *and,* or at the end of a word, is pronounced like the *e* in *he: y,* **hay, doy.**

Z

z is pronounced like an *s:* **azul, pizarra.** In Spain, z is pronounced like English *th.*

The English *z* sound is produced in Spanish by an **s** or **z** (only by the **s** in Spain) before a voiced consonant (**b, d, g, l, m, n**): **desde, mismo, durazno.**

The following common English combinations do not exist in Spanish: *gh, ny, ph, sh, th.* The only consonants that may be doubled in Spanish are **c** (**acción**) and **n** (**ennoblecer**). **ll** and **rr** are letters in their own right and should not be confused with **l** and **r.**

See also ACCENT MARK, ALPHABET, DIERESIS, DIPHTHONGS, DIVISION OF WORDS INTO SYLLABLES (SYLLABIFICATION), and ELISION.

A

The preposition **a** is used in Spanish in a variety of situations. Most often, it translates *to*. However, in certain constructions and set expressions it may be translated as *at, from, on, in,* or *by.* In some cases, it is not translated at all and has no English equivalent. The following are the most common uses of the preposition **a.**

1. Personal *a*

When the direct object of a verb is a noun referring to a specific person or persons, it is preceded by a *personal* **a** that does not translate into English.

Conozco **a** su papá.	*I know his father.*
¿Llevas **a** Tina?	*Are you taking Tina?*

Alguien *(somebody)*, **nadie** *(nobody)*, and **quién** *(whom)* require a personal **a** when used as direct objects. **Alguno(s)** *(anyone, some)* and **ninguno** *(no one, none)* are also preceded by **a** when they refer to persons and are direct objects.

¿Oyes **a alguien?**	*Do you hear **anyone**?*
No oigo **a nadie.**	*I don't hear **anyone**.*
¿**A quién** buscas?	***Whom** are you looking for?*

Geographical places and pets may be personified and take the personal **a.**

Olga ama **a** su perro.	*Olga loves her dog.*
Ella extraña mucho **a** Cuba.	*She misses Cuba a lot.*

The personal **a** is not normally used after **tener** or when the direct object is an indefinite person or a collective noun that denotes a general class rather than particular individuals.

Tengo tres primos.	*I **have** three cousins.*
Necesito **una secretaria** que sepa el español.	*I need **a secretary** who knows Spanish.*
Necesitan **más gente** allí.	*They need **more people** there.*

When **tener** means *to hold someone* or *to have somebody restricted or confined,* the personal **a** is used.

Tengo a mi hija en la guardería.	*I **have** my daughter in day care.*

2. *a* to Distinguish a Subject from a Direct Object

When both the direct object and the subject refer to things in such a way that ambiguity could result, an **a** may be used before the object. The **a** is not translated to English in such instances.

El tren alcanzó **al** carro.	*The train caught up with the car.*

3. *a* with Verbs of Movement or Progression

The preposition **a** is commonly associated with movement or progression toward a place or into an activity. It is used before places and infinitives that follow verbs indicating movement (**ir, venir, volver,** etc.) and before infinitives that follow verbs indicating progression into an activity (**aprender, comenzar, empezar, enseñar,** etc.).

Vienen **a** trabajar.	*They are coming to work.*
El volvió **a** casa.	*He returned home.*
Aprendiste **a** bailar.	*You learned to dance.*
Se puso **a** jugar.	*He began to play.*

4. Other Verbs Usually Followed by *a*

acercarse a	*to approach*
acostumbrarse a	*to become accustomed to*
asistir a	*to attend*
asomarse a	*to look or peek through*
atreverse a	*to dare*
condenar a	*to condemn to*
dar a	*to face, look out on*
detenerse a	*to stop to*
dirigirse a	*to address, go toward*
echar a	*to begin*
jugar a	*to play*
negarse a	*to refuse to*
obligar a	*to oblige*
oler a	*to smell like*
parecerse a	*to look like*
ponerse a	*to begin*
resolverse a	*to decide to*
saber a	*to taste like*
sonar a	*to sound like*
subir a	*to get on*
volver a	*to . . . again*

These verbs require **a** only when followed by an infinitive or an object.

¿**Asistió a** la reunión?	***Did he attend** the meeting?*
Sí, **asistió.**	*Yes, **he attended.***

¿Se **negó a** decirte?	*Did she refuse to tell you?*
Sí, se **negó.**	*Yes, she refused.*

5. *a* with Indirect Object Nouns

The preposition **a** is required before nouns serving as indirect objects and in such cases may mean *to, for, from,* or *on.*

Le gustaba la casa **a** María.	*María liked the house. (The house was pleasing **to** María.)*
Le compré estas flores **a** mi mamá.	*I bought these flowers **for** my mother.*
Ella les puso los zapatos **a** los niños.	*She put the shoes **on** the children.*
Le quitaron el pasaporte **a** Beto.	*They took the passport **from** Beto.*
Un Chevy le gana **a** un Ford.	*A Chevy beats a Ford.*

6. *a* with Expressions of Measurement

The preposition **a** translates *at* before expressions of measurement (price, speed, time, etc.). In most other cases, **en** translates *at.*

a la una, **a** las dos, etc.	*at one o'clock, at two o'clock, etc.*
a (al) mediodía	*at noon*
a diez pesos el kilo	*at ten pesos a kilo*
a cien kilómetros por hora	*at 100 km per hour*

7. *a* to Convey *on*

The following expressions use **a** to translate *on.* In most other cases, **en** translates *on.*

a bordo	*on board*
a caballo	*on horseback*
a la derecha	*on (to) the right*

a la izquierda	*on (to) the left*
a pie	*on foot*
a tiempo	*on time*

8. *a* to Convey *by*

Expressions of manner or means use **a** to translate *by*.

Hecho **a** mano.	*Made by hand.*
Los escribe **a** máquina.	*He types them (by machine).*
Poco **a** poco.	*Little by little.*

9. Other Common Expressions with *a*

a causa de	*because of*
a eso de	*at about*
a gatas	*crawling, on hands and knees*
a la larga	*in the long run*
a lo largo de	*along*
a lo lejos	*in the distance*
a menudo	*often*
a pesar de	*in spite of*
a poco de	*a short while after*
a saltos	*jumping, by leaps*
a solas	*alone*
a través de	*through, by means of*
al	*upon (followed by an infinitive)*
al fin	*finally*

A + EL: *See AL: A + EL*

A.M.

A.M. is **de la mañana.**

Salgo a la una **de la mañana.**	*I leave at one A.M.*

A MENOS QUE *(UNLESS)*

A menos que is always followed by a verb in the subjunctive mood.

A menos que él pague, no voy.	*Unless he pays, I'm not going.*

See PRESENT TENSE SUBJUNCTIVE.

ABBREVIATIONS

Here is a list of some of the most common Spanish abbreviations and their English equivalents.

Abbreviation	Literal Meaning	English
adj.	adjunto	*enclosed*
a. de J. C.	antes de Jesucristo	B.C. *(before Christ)*
apdo.	apartado postal	P.O. *box*
Av.	avenida	*avenue*
Cía	compañía	*company*
cm.	centímetro	*centimeter*
D.	don	*Sir*
Da.	doña	*Madam*
d. de J. C.	después de Jesucristo	A.D.
D.F.	Distrito Federal	*Federal District (Mexico)*
Dr(a).	doctor(a)	*doctor*

Abbreviation	Literal Meaning	English
E.	este	*east, eastern*
EEUU	Estados Unidos	*United States*
esq.	esquina	*corner*
f.c.	ferrocarril	*railroad*
fe.	femenino	*feminine*
Fr.	fraile	*friar, brother*
Gral.	general	*general*
Hno(s).	hermanos	*brothers*
Ing.	ingeniero	*engineer*
kg.	kilogramo	*kilogram*
km.	kilómetro	*kilometer*
l.	litro	*liter*
Lic.	licenciado	*attorney*
m.	masculino	*masculine*
N.	norte	*north, northern*
núm.	número	*number*
O.	oeste	*west, western*
OEA	Organización de Estados Americanos	*Organization of American States (OAS)*
ONU	Organización de Naciones Unidas	*United Nations (UN)*
OTAN	Organización del Tratado del Norte	*North Atlantic Treaty Organization (NATO)*
Pag(s).	página(s)	*page(s)*
P.D.	posdata	*P.S. (in letters)*
Prof(a).	profesor(a)	*professor*

Abbreviation	Literal Meaning	English
q.e.p.d.	que en paz descanse	*Rest in peace*
S.	sur	*south, southern*
S.A.	Sociedad Anónima	*Inc.*
Sr.	señor	*Mr., sir*
Sra.	señora	*Mrs., ma'am*
Srta.	señorita	*Miss*
Tel.	teléfono	*telephone*
Ud., Vd.	usted	*you (singular)*
Uds., Vds.	ustedes	*you (plural)*
v.	véase	*see*

ABIERTO

Past participle of **abrir** *(to open)*.

ABSOLUTE SUPERLATIVE: *See VERY.*

ACÁ: *See HERE:* ACÁ *VS.* AQUÍ.

ACABAR DE

The present tense of **acabar** + **de** + an infinitive translates *have just* or *has just*. In the imperfect tense it means *had just*.

Acaban de salir.	*They **have just** left.*
Acaba de comprarlo.	*He **has just** bought it.*
Yo **acababa de** llegar.	*I **had just** arrived.*

Without **de, acabar** means *to finish, complete,* or *end.*

Acabó su tarea.	*He **finished** his homework.*

ACCENT MARK

Most Spanish words do not require an accent mark (´) because they follow two simple rules that determine pronunciation. In general, words that need an accent mark require one because they deviate from these rules. Accent marks appear only over vowels.

RULE #1: Words ending in a vowel, -n, or -s.

Words that end in a *vowel* or **-n** or **-s** normally have the stress on the next-to-last syllable and do not take an accent mark: **ma-le-ta, pa-lan-ca, jo-ven.**
If the stress is on any other syllable, an accent mark must be placed over the stressed vowel: **so-fá, ca-fé, tam-bién, mé-di-co, jó-ve-nes.**

All words ending in **-ión** are stressed on the last syllable and consequently have an accent mark on the **ó (pasión, lección, acción)**, but the plural forms do not **(pasiones, lecciones, acciones)**.

RULE #2: Words ending in consonants other than -n or -s.

Words that end in a *consonant* other than **-n** or **-s** normally have the stress on the last syllable and do not require a written accent: **ho-tel, pa-pel, ver-dad.**
If the stress is on any other syllable, an accent mark must be placed over the stressed vowel: **fá-cil, lá-piz.**

All Spanish words that are stressed before the next-to-last syllable require an accent mark over the stressed vowel: **lá-gri-ma, lin-dí-si-ma, mé-di-co, re-lám-pa-go.**

All Spanish words that have a stressed **i** or **u** next to an **a, e,** or **o** require an accent mark over the **i** or **u: te-ní-a, grú-a, rí-o.**

Homonyms

With some Spanish homonyms, the accent mark distinguishes meaning.

aquél*	*that one*	aquel*	*that*
aún	*still, yet*	aun	*even*
dé	*give*	de	*of, from*
él	*he, him*	el	*the*

más	*more*	mas	*but*
mí	*me*	mi	*my*
ó	*or (between numbers)*	o	*or*
sé	*I know, be*	se†	†
sí	*yes* (See *REFLEXIVE PRONOUNS*)	si	*if*
sólo	*only*	solo	*alone*
té	*tea*	te	*you*
tú	*you*	tu	*your*

*Other demonstratives follow this pattern. *See DEMONSTRATIVE ADJEC-TIVES AND PRONOUNS.*

†*See REFLEXIVE PRONOUNS and INDIRECT OBJECT PRONOUNS.*

The interrogatives (**cuál, dónde, cuándo, qué,** etc.) also require accent marks. *See INTERROGATIVES.*

ACTIVE VOICE

The *active voice* indicates that the subject acts rather than is acted upon.

Subject Acts (active voice)	Subject Acted Upon (passive voice)
El niño **abrió** la ventana.	La ventana **fue abierta** por el niño.
*The child **opened** the window.*	*The window **was opened** by the child.*
Ella **hará** los tamales.	Los tamales **serán hechos** por ella.
*She **will make** the tamales.*	*The tamales **will be made** by her.*

See PASSIVE VOICE.

ADDRESS (MAIL)

Addresses in the Spanish-speaking world have the name of the street first and the street number following.

¿Cuál es su dirección?	*What is your address?*
Vivo en (la calle) **Buena Vista 921.**	*I live at **921 Buena Vista** (St.)*

ADJECTIVE CLAUSES

An *adjective clause* is a group of words that contains a subject and verb (predicate) but does not express a complete thought. The clause is used as an adjective to modify a noun or a pronoun.

El hombre **que habló** es mi abuelo.	*The man **who spoke** is my grandfather.*

See PRESENT TENSE SUBJUNCTIVE and RELATIVE PRONOUNS.

ADJECTIVES

Forms

All descriptive adjectives have singular and plural forms, and many have separate masculine and feminine forms as well. For a discussion of gender, *see NOUNS.*

Adjectives whose masculine singular form ends in **-o (alto, barato, negro)** have four forms, and they must agree with the noun they modify.

el edificio **amarillo**	*the **yellow** building*
los edificios **amarillos**	*the **yellow** buildings*
la casa **amarilla**	*the **yellow** house*
las casas **amarillas**	*the **yellow** houses*

Most adjectives whose masculine singular form ends in a *consonant* **(feliz, azul)** or in a vowel other than **-o (verde, inteligente)** do not have separate masculine and feminine forms and thus have only two forms.

Adjectives are pluralized the same as nouns. *See NOUNS.*

la camisa **azul**	*the **blue** shirt*
las camisas **azules**	*the **blue** shirts*

el coche **azul**	*the **blue** car*
los coches **azules**	*the **blue** cars*
la corbata **verde**	*the **green** tie*
las corbatas **verdes**	*the **green** ties*
el sombrero **verde**	*the **green** hat*
los sombreros **verdes**	*the **green** hats*
Feliz Navidad	***Merry** Christmas*
Felices Pascuas	***Happy** Holidays*

Adjectives of nationality whose masculine singular form ends in a consonant (**español, francés, alemán**) add the endings **-a, -es,** or **-as** to form their feminine and plural forms: **española, españoles, españolas** *(Spanish)*. Adjectives of nationality whose singular form ends in **-e** have only two forms: **canadiense, canadienses** *(Canadian)*.

el coche **japonés**	*the **Japanese** car*
la motocicleta **japonesa**	*the **Japanese** motorcycle*
los coches **japoneses**	*the **Japanese** cars*
las motocicletas **japonesas**	*the **Japanese** motorcycles*
el hombre **canadiense**	*the **Canadian** man*
la mujer **canadiense**	*the **Canadian** woman*
los hombres **canadienses**	*the **Canadian** men*
las mujeres **canadienses**	*the **Canadian** women*

Adjectives that have masculine singular forms ending in **-án, -ón,** or **-ín** drop the accent mark and add **-a, -es,** or **-as** to form their feminine and plural forms. The same endings are added to adjectives whose masculine singular form ends in **-or** provided that they are derived from verbs (**hablador, trabajador**) and do not have a comparative value. Those that are not derived from verbs and that usually have a comparative value (**menor, mayor, mejor, peor, superior, inferior, interior, exterior, posterior**) have only two forms and are made plural by adding **-es.**

un **niño llorón**	a **crybaby** (little boy)
una **niña llorona**	a **crybaby** (little girl)
los **niños llorones**	**crybabies** (children, little boys)
las **niñas lloronas**	**crybabies** (little girls)
un hombre **hablador**	a **talkative** man
una mujer **habladora**	a **talkative** woman
unos hombres **habladores**	**talkative** men
unas mujeres **habladoras**	**talkative** women
mi hermano **mayor**	my **older** brother
mi hermana **mayor**	my **older** sister
mis hermanos **mayores**	my **older** brothers
mis hermanas **mayores**	my **older** sisters

Adjectives modifying two or more nouns of different gender take the masculine plural form.

La pluma y **el libro** son **nuevos.**	**The pen** and **the book** are **new.**

Placement

1. *Descriptive adjectives* normally follow the noun they modify. However, adjectives that describe qualities that the noun is expected to have may precede it. Adjectives that are modified by adverbs must be placed after the noun they modify.

el libro **verde**	the **green** book
unos problemas **fáciles**	some **easy** problems
una camisa **barata**	a **cheap** shirt
la **blanca** nieve	the **white** snow
los **altos** picos	the **high** peaks
unos picos **muy altos**	some **very high** peaks

2. *Adjectives of quantity* (limiting) precede the noun.

muchos secretos	*many secrets*
varias revistas	*several magazines*

3. The last adjective in a series of two or more is preceded by **y**.

Es una mujer **alta y elegante.**	*She is a **tall, elegant** woman.*

4. A few adjectives (**bueno, malo, mejor,** and **peor**) may be placed either before or after the noun without any significant change in meaning. The placement after the noun makes the adjective slightly more emphatic.

Son **buenos** estudiantes.	*They are **good** students.*
Son estudiantes **buenos.**	*They are **(really) good** students.*

5. Certain adjectives change meaning depending on whether they precede or follow the noun.

Adjective	*Preceding*	*Following*
antiguo	*old (former)*	*old, ancient*
gran(de)	*great*	*large*
mismo	*same*	*himself, herself, etc.*
nuevo	*new (different)*	*new*
pobre	*poor (unfortunate)*	*poor (without money)*
propio	*own*	*proper*
único	*only*	*unique*
viejo	*old (long-time)*	*old (elderly)*

La **misma** profesora me dijo.	*The **same** professor told me.*
La profesora **misma** me dijo.	*The professor **herself** told me.*
Mi **pobre** tío tiene cáncer.	*My **poor** uncle has cancer.*
El hombre **pobre** no tiene coche.	*The **poor** man doesn't have a car.*

6. Some adjectives have reduced or shortened forms (apocopation): **Santo** *(Saint)* becomes **San** before all masculine names except **Tomás** and **Domingo**. **Grande** *(large)* is shortened to **gran** before singular nouns (masculine or feminine) and means *great*. Some adjectives (**alguno, bueno, malo, ninguno, postrero, primero, tercero,** and **uno**) drop the **-o** when placed before masculine singular nouns. In all other instances their forms are regular.

algún día	*some day*
un buen muchacho	*a good boy*
un gran futbolista	*a great soccer player*

See also BUENO, COMPARATIVES, DEMONSTRATIVE ADJECTIVES AND PRONOUNS, and POSSESSIVE ADJECTIVES.

ADJECTIVES USED AS NOUNS

Adjectives are commonly used as nouns by dropping the noun but retaining the article. Spanish does not use an equivalent for the word *one(s)* in this construction. When used as a noun, an adjective must agree in gender and number with the noun it represents.

Los discos nuevos son mejores.	*The new records are better.*
Los nuevos son mejores.	*The new ones are better.*
La casa blanca es cara.	*The white house is expensive.*
La blanca es cara.	*The white one is expensive.*

ADÓNDE: *See INTERROGATIVES.*

ADVERBIAL CLAUSES

An *adverbial clause* is a group of words that contains a subject and verb (predicate) but does not express a complete thought. The clause is used as an adverb to modify a verb.

Yo le dije **cuando lo vi.**	*I told him **when I saw him.***

See PRESENT TENSE SUBJUNCTIVE.

ADVERBS

Adverbs modify or limit the meaning of a verb, an adjective, or another adverb. Unlike adjectives, they do not change form to agree with the word they modify. The most common adverbial ending in Spanish is **-mente**. It is added to the feminine adjective form and corresponds to the English *-ly*.

If **-mente** is added to an adjective that ends in **-o** (such as **violento**), the **-o** is changed to **a** before adding **-mente** (**violentamente**). Only the last of two or more adverbs in a series ends in **-mente**; the feminine form of the adjective is used with the others. Adjectives that require an accent mark retain the accent mark when **-mente** is added.

Él lo hizo **fácilmente**.	*He did it **easily**.*
Adelita está **locamente** enamorada del sargento.	*Adelita is **madly** in love with the sergeant.*
Habló **clara, directa y rápidamente**.	*He spoke **clearly, directly, and quickly**.*

Frequently **con** + a noun substitutes for an adverb.

Me contestó **cariñosamente**.	*She answered me **affectionately**.*
Me contestó **con cariño**.	*She answered me **affectionately**.*

AFFIRMATIVE AND NEGATIVE INDEFINITES

Affirmative		*Negative*	
algo	*something, anything*	nada	*nothing, anything*
alguien	*someone, somebody, anyone, anybody*	nadie	*nobody, anybody, no one, anyone*
algún	*some*	ningún	*no, (not) any*
alguno(a)	*some*	ninguno(a)	*no, none, (not) any*
algunos(as)	*some*	ningunos(as)	*no, (not) any*
o . . . o	*either . . . or*	ni . . . ni	*neither . . . nor either . . . or*

siempre	*always*	nunca (jamás)	*never, ever*
también	*also, too*	tampoco	*neither, either*

No + verb + negative expression is the same as negative expression + verb.

No quiere **nada.**	*He doesn't want **anything**.*
Nada quiere.	*He doesn't want **anything**.*
No duermen **nunca.**	*They **never** sleep.*
Nunca duermen.	*They **never** sleep.*

In Spanish, negative and affirmative expressions are not normally used together in the same clause. This may lead to multiple negative expressions in the same sentence.

Nunca le dice **nada** a **nadie.**	*He **never** says **anything** to **anyone**.*
Yo **no** le pido **nada** a **nadie nunca tampoco.**	*I **don't ever** ask **anyone** for **anything either**.*

When used as direct objects, **alguien** and **nadie** are preceded by **a.**

No conozco **a nadie** aquí.	*I don't know **anybody** here.*
¿Conoces **a alguien?**	*Do you know **anybody?***

Negatives are used with **más que** *(more than).*

más que nada	*more than anything*
más que nadie	*more than anybody*
más que nunca	*more than ever*

The plural forms **ningunas** and **ningunos** exist, but the singular forms **ningún, ninguna,** and **ninguno** usually replace them and may translate as the plural in English. **Ninguno** becomes **ningún** before a masculine singular noun.

No trajo **ningún** refresco.	*He didn't bring **any** soft drinks.*
No corté **ninguna** flor.	*I didn't cut **any** flowers.*

¿Cuántos refrescos bebiste?	*How many soft drinks did you drink?*
No bebí **ninguno.**	*I didn't drink any.*

O ... o	Ni ... ni	Tampoco

Quiere cerveza **o** vino.	*He wants beer or wine.*
Quiere **o** cerveza **o** vino.	*He wants either beer or wine.*
No quiere cerveza **ni** vino.	*He doesn't want beer or wine.*
No quiere **ni** cerveza **ni** vino.	*He doesn't want either beer or wine.*
No quiere cerveza. **No** quiere vino **tampoco.**	*He doesn't want beer. He doesn't want wine either.*

AGO

Hace + time period is used to translate *ago.* When **hace** is used with a verb to express *ago,* the verb is in the preterit or imperfect tense. In these constructions, **hace** may appear at the beginning of the sentence or after the verb.

¿Cuándo llegaste?	*When did you arrive?*
Hace una hora.	*An hour ago.*
Hace cinco años que lo **compré.**	*I bought it five years ago.*
Lo **compré hace** cinco años.	*I bought it five years ago.*

AGREEMENT

Several types of grammatical agreement occur in Spanish: A verb agrees in person (**yo, tú,** etc.) and number (singular or plural) with its subject; an adjective agrees in number and gender (masculine or feminine) with the noun it modifies; and a pronoun often agrees in number and gender with the noun it represents.

AGUDA (PALABRA)

A **palabra aguda** is a word whose stress is on the last syllable (pa**pel**, fe**liz**, apren**dió**).
See ACCENT MARK.

AHÍ: *See THERE:* AHÍ, ALLÍ, ALLÁ.

AL: A + EL

The combination of **a** *(to)* + **el** *(the)* must render the contraction **al** unless **el** is part of a proper noun.

¿Vas **al** partido?	*Are you going **to the** game?*
No vi **al** profesor.	*I didn't see **the** professor.*
Fui **a El** Paso.	*I went **to El** Paso.*

However, **a** *(to)* + **él** *(him)* do not contract.

Se la di **a él.**	*I gave it **to him.***
¿Le escribiste **a él?**	*Did you write **to him**?*

AL *(ON, UPON)*

Al meaning **on, upon,** or **when** is always followed by an infinitive.

Al pagar la cuenta, salió.	***Upon paying** the bill, she left.*
Al recibir las malas noticias, se desmayó.	***Upon receiving** the bad news, he fainted.*

ALGO: *See AFFIRMATIVE AND NEGATIVE INDEFINITES.*

ALGUIEN: *See AFFIRMATIVE AND NEGATIVE INDEFINITES.*

ALLÁ: *See THERE:* AHÍ, ALLÍ, ALLÁ.

ALLÍ: *See THERE:* AHÍ, ALLÍ, ALLÁ.

ALPHABET

Letter	Name	Letter	Name
a	a	n	ene
b	be, be grande	ñ	eñe
c	ce	o	o
ch	che	p	pe
d	de	q	cu
e	e	r	ere
f	efe	rr	erre
g	ge	s	ese
h	hache	t	te
i	i	u	u
j	jota	v	ve, uve, v chica
k	ka	w	doble u, doble v
l	ele	x	equis
ll	elle	y	y griega
m	eme	z	zeta

AND: Y VS. E

Before words beginning with **i** or **hi** (except **hie-**), *and* is expressed with **e.** In all other instances, **y** expresses *and.*

Olga **e** Isabel	*Olga **and** Isabel*
padre **e** hijo	*father **and** son*

Isabel **y** Olga	*Isabel **and** Olga*
nieve **y** hielo	*snow **and** ice*

ANDAR

Irregular Forms
Preterit: **anduve, anduviste, anduvo, anduvimos, anduvisteis, anduvieron**
Imperfect subjunctive: **anduviera, anduvieras,** etc.; **anduviese, anduvieses,** etc.

Andar generally means *to walk or ride,* but it may also mean *to run* or *to work* in the context of appliances or machinery. **Andar** may also translate *to go* or *to be,* especially when combined with a present participle.

Voy **a andar** al centro.	*I'm going to **walk** downtown.*
El coche no **anda.**	*The car doesn't **run.***
José **anda** en bicicleta.	*José **is riding** his bicycle.*
Él **anda pidiendo** dinero.	*He **is going around asking for** money.*

To *run* and to *work* (for people) are **correr** and **trabajar.**

No **trabajo** el sábado.	*I don't **work** on Saturday.*
Paco **corre** dos millas.	*Paco **runs** two miles.*

ANTE/ANTES (DE): *See BEFORE:* ANTE *VS.* ANTES (DE).

ANY

Any is usually not expressed in Spanish, especially in questions. In the negative, **ningún, ninguna,** or **ninguno** may express *any.*

¿Tienes dinero?	*Do you have **any** money?*
No quiere **ningún** consejo.	*He doesn't want **any** advice.*

See CUALQUIER(A) *and AFFIRMATIVE AND NEGATIVE INDEFINITES.*

APOCOPATION: *See* BUEN(O).

APOSTROPHE: *See* DE *(SPECIAL USES) and POSSESSION WITH* DE.

APPLY: APLICAR(SE) *VS.* SOLICITAR

For conjugation of **aplicar,** *see* -CAR *VERBS.*

Solicitar translates *to apply for* a job, scholarship, and the like, whereas **aplicar** translates *to apply something,* such as cream, ointment, or pressure. **Aplicarse** expresses *to apply oneself.*

¿Vas a **solicitar** otro puesto?	*Are you going **to apply for** another job?*
Le **aplicaron** presión a la herida.	*They **applied** pressure to the wound.*
Se **aplicó** a sus estudios.	*He **applied** himself to his studies.*

AQUEL (AQUELLO, AQUELLA, AQUELLAS, AQUELLOS): *See DEMONSTRATIVE ADJECTIVES AND PRONOUNS.*

ARTICLES: *See DEFINITE ARTICLES, INDEFINITE ARTICLES, and* LO.

AS . . . AS (TAN . . . COMO)

Dora es **tan** alta **como** Rita.	*Dora is **as** tall **as** Rita.*

AS (SO) MUCH/MANY AS (TANTO[S] COMO)

Tanto and **tanta** express *as (so) much,* and **tantos** and **tantas** express *as many.* They are usually followed by **como** *(as).*

Toma **tanta** leche **como** un bebé.	*He drinks **as much** milk **as** a baby.*
¿Tienes **tantos** amigos **como** tu hermano?	*Do you have **as many** friends **as** your brother?*
Hay **tanto** trabajo que hacer.	*There is **so much** work to do.*

When verbs are compared, **tanto como** follows the verb and translates *as much as.*

Ella estudia **tanto como** tú.	*She studies **as much as** you do.*

ASK: PEDIR VS. PREGUNTAR

To ask in the sense of *request* or *ask for* is expressed by **pedir,** and *to ask* meaning *inquire* or *ask about* is expressed by **preguntar.** When asking someone to do something, **pedir** is used. **Preguntar** may be followed by **por** *(about)*, but **pedir** is not followed by **por.**

Me **pidió** dinero.	*He asked me for money.*
Me **preguntó por** el dinero.	*He asked me about the money.*
Me **pide** que vaya con ella.	*She asks me to go with her.*

For conjugation of **pedir,** *see STEM-CHANGING VERBS:* -IR.

ATTEND: ASISTIR VS. ATENDER

Asistir a means *to attend* in the sense of *to be present,* and **atender** is *to attend to* in the sense of *to take care of.*

No **asistí a** la conferencia anoche.	*I didn't attend the lecture last night.*
Me **atienden** bien aquí.	*They give me good service here.*

For conjugation of **atender,** *see STEM-CHANGING VERBS:* -AR *AND* -ER.

AUGMENTATIVES: *See SUFFIXES.*

AUNQUE (ALTHOUGH, THOUGH, EVEN THOUGH, EVEN IF)

When the notion of *may* is conveyed, **aunque** *(though, although, even though, even if)* is followed by a verb in the subjunctive mood. When not conveying the notion of *may,* a verb in the indicative mood follows **aunque.**

Aunque salgas temprano, no vas a llegar a tiempo.	*Although you may leave early, you're not going to arrive on time.*
Aunque siempre **sales** temprano, nunca llegas a tiempo.	*Although you always leave early, you never arrive on time.*

-AZO: *See SUFFIXES.*

B

BE: *See* SER *VS.* ESTAR.

BECAUSE (OF): PORQUE VS. A CAUSA DE (POR)

Porque means *because* and is followed by a clause that contains a conjugated verb. **A causa de** means *because of* and is followed by a noun. **Por** also means *because* or *because of* and may be followed by a noun or an infinitive.

No voy a Kmart **porque** hace mal tiempo.	*I'm not going to Kmart **because** the weather is bad.*
No voy a Kmart **a causa del** tiempo.	*I'm not going to Kmart **because of** the weather.*
Juan no va a comer **porque** está cansado.	*Juan isn't going to eat **because** he is tired.*
Juan no va a comer **por** estar cansado.	*Juan isn't going to eat **because** he is tired.*

BECOME (GET)

Ponerse + adjective expresses *to become* in the context of a temporary change.

Se puso roja.	*She **became (got)** red.*

Volverse + adjective is used to indicate a more deep-seated change.

Se volvió loco.	*He **went (became)** crazy.*

Hacerse + adjective or noun is *to become* as a result of one's efforts.

Se hicieron ricos.	*They **became** rich.*
Se hizo ingeniero.	*He **became** an engineer.*

Llegar a ser is *to become* after a gradual process leading to a positive culmination.

Llegó a ser gobernador.	*He **became** governor.*

Many reflexive verbs convey *become* or *get*.

Te enfermarás.	*You will **get (become)** sick.*
Se emborrachan.	*They **get (become)** drunk.*
Nos vestimos.	*We **got** dressed.*
¿Te enojaste?	*Did you **get (become)** angry?*
Me cansé.	*I **got (became)** tired.*

BEFORE: ANTE *VS.* ANTES (DE)

Before meaning *in the presence of* is translated by **ante**; *before* in a sequential or chronological sense is translated by **antes (de).**

Antes de su juicio, el preso tendrá que comparecer **ante** el juez.	***Before** his trial, the prisoner will have to appear **before** the judge.*

BEST

Best is expressed by **mejor(es)** and is usually preceded by a definite article. **De,** not **en,** expresses *in* after **mejor(es).**

Son los **mejores** atletas **de** la ciudad.	*They are the **best** athletes **in** the city.*

BETTER

Better is expressed by **mejor(es)** and is followed by **que** *(than)* in comparisons.

| Las verduras crudas son **mejores que** las verduras cocidas. | *Raw vegetables are **better than** cooked vegetables.* |

BUSCAR *(TO LOOK FOR)*

For conjugation, *see* -CAR *VERBS.*
Buscar means *to look for* and is not followed by either **por** or **para.**

| Raúl está **buscando** su ropa interior. | *Raúl is **looking for** his underwear.* |

BUT: PERO *VS.* SINO

Pero is the usual translation of *but.* **Sino** and **sino que** are used after a negative followed by a contradicting affirmative. **Sino que** is followed by a conjugated verb and introduces a clause. **Mas** may substitute for **pero.**

Estudia ciencias **pero** no estudia idiomas.	*He studies sciences, **but** he doesn't study languages.*
No estudia ciencias, **pero** va a la universidad.	*He doesn't study sciences, **but** he goes to the university.*
No estudia ciencias **sino** idiomas.	*He doesn't study sciences **but** languages.*
No estudia ciencias **sino que** estudia idiomas.	*He doesn't study sciences, **but** he studies languages.*
Va a estudiar ciencias, **mas** no quiere.	*He is going to study sciences, **but** he doesn't want to.*

BUEN(O)

Bueno *(good)* apocopates (is reduced) to **buen** before a masculine singular noun. Other forms of this adjective do not change, regardless of position.

Necesito un **buen** puesto.	*I need a **good** job.*
Necesito un puesto **bueno.**	*I need a **good** job.*
Encontré una **buena** revista.	*I found a **good** magazine.*
Encontré una revista **buena.**	*I found a **good** magazine.*

Other adjectives that follow the pattern of **bueno** include **alguno** *(some)*, **malo** *(bad, sick)*, **ninguno** *(none, not any)*, **postrero** *(last)*, **primero** *(first)*, **tercero** *(third)*, and **uno** *(one)*.

BY

En or **por** translates *by* in the context of means of transportation.

Llegó **por** tren y regresó **en** avión.	*He came by train, and he returned by plane.*

By meaning *not later than* is expressed by **para.**

Habré terminado **para** mañana.	*I will have finished by tomorrow.*
Ya habían salido **para** las once.	*They had already left by eleven o'clock.*

By meaning *manufactured (made) by* is **a.**

Mi bolsa fue hecha **a** mano.	*My purse was made by hand.*

By meaning *near* is **cerca de.**

Vive **cerca de** mí.	*He lives by me.*

By with the passive voice is translated by **por.**

La carta fue escrita **por** Pilar.	*The letter was written by Pilar.*

A present participle may include *by* in its meaning.

Trabajando los fines de semana, Ramón ganará el dinero que necesita.	*By working weekends, Ramón will earn the money he needs.*
Saliendo temprano, llegaremos al mediodía.	*By leaving early, we will arrive at noon.*

CABER *(TO FIT)*

Irregular Forms
Present Indicative: **quepo,** cabes, cabe, cabemos, cabéis, caben
Preterit: **cupe, cupiste, cupo, cupimos, cupisteis, cupieron**
Future: **cabré, cabrás, cabrá, cabremos, cabréis, cabrán**
Conditional: **cabría, cabrías, cabría, cabríamos, cabríais, cabrían**
Present Subjunctive: **quepa, quepas, quepa, quepamos, quepáis, quepan**
Imperfect Subjunctive: **cupiera,** etc.; **cupiese,** etc.

CAER *(TO FALL)*

Irregular Forms
Present Indicative: **caigo,** caes, cae, caemos, caéis, caen
Preterit: caí, **caíste, cayó, caímos, cayeron**
Present Subjunctive: **caiga, caigas, caiga, caigamos, caigáis, caigan**
Imperfect Subjunctive: **cayera,** etc.; **cayese,** etc.
Present Participle: **cayendo**
Past Participle: **caído**

CAN: See PODER

CAPITALIZATION

Spanish uses fewer capital letters than English. Days of the week, months, languages, religions, and adjectives of nationality are not capitalized in Spanish.

Hoy es **martes.**	*Today is **Tuesday.***
Regresan en **abril.**	*They return in **April.***

No hablan **inglés**.	*They don't speak **English**.*
Es **católica**.	*She is **Catholic**.*
Ellos son **franceses**.	*They are **French**.*

The first word of a sentence and proper nouns (names of people, pets, cities, states, countries, rivers, mountains, etc.) are capitalized.

El perro se llama **O**so.	*The dog's name is Oso.*
Es de **E**l Cajón, California.	*He is from El Cajón, California.*
El río **A**mazonas comienza en los Andes en el **P**erú.	*The Amazon River begins in the Andes in Peru.*

Only the first word and proper nouns are capitalized in the titles of books, plays, movies, songs, and the like.

El laberinto de la soledad	*The Labyrinth of Solitude*
La muerte de Artemio Cruz	*The Death of Artemio Cruz*
Como agua para chocolate	*Like Water for Chocolate*

Personal titles (**señor, señora, doctor, general,** etc.) and **usted** and **ustedes** are not capitalized unless they are abbreviated.

el **Sr.** López	*Mr. López*
la señorita Miranda	*Miss Miranda*
el **Dr.** Ruiz y **Ud.**	*Doctor Ruiz and you*

-CAR *VERBS*

Verbs ending in **-car** change the **-c-** to **-qu-** in the **yo** form of the preterit tense, in all forms of the present subjunctive, and in **usted** and **ustedes** commands as well as in negative **tú** commands.

BUSCAR *(TO LOOK FOR)*
Irregular Forms
Preterit: **busqué**, buscaste, buscó, buscamos, buscasteis, buscaron
Present Subjunctive: **busque, busques, busque, busquemos, busquéis, busquen**
Commands: **busque** Ud., **busquen** Uds., no **busques** tú

Other common **-car** verbs include **acercarse** *(to approach)*, **atacar** *(to attack)*, **colocar** *(to place)*, **equivocarse** *(to be mistaken)*, **explicar** *(to explain)*, **pescar** *(to fish)*, **platicar** *(to chat)*, **practicar** *(to practice)*, **sacar** *(to take out)*, **significar** *(to mean)*, and **tocar** *(to play, touch)*.

CARDINAL NUMBERS

1	uno	21	veintiuno
2	dos	22	veintidós
3	tres	23	veintitrés
4	cuatro	24	veinticuatro
5	cinco	25	veinticinco
6	seis	26	veintiséis
7	siete	27	veintisiete
8	ocho	28	veintiocho
9	nueve	29	veintinueve
10	diez	30	treinta
11	once	31	treinta y uno
12	doce	32	treinta y dos
13	trece	40	cuarenta
14	catorce	50	cincuenta
15	quince	60	sesenta
16	dieciséis	70	setenta
17	diecisiete	80	ochenta
18	dieciocho	90	noventa
19	diecinueve	100	cien
20	veinte	100	ciento

Most cardinal numbers are invariable, that is, they have one form only (**seis, siete, ocho**). Numbers 16–29 may also be written as three words (**diez y seis, diez y siete**). Numbers 31–99 *must* be written as three words (**treinta y uno, treinta y dos**).

Any combination of *one* has three forms: **-un, -una,** and **-uno. Uno** is used in counting and stands alone. **Un** is used only before a masculine noun. **Una** is used before a feminine noun and may also stand alone.

un caballo	*one horse*	cincuenta y **un** mosquitos	
		*Fifty-**one** mosquitos*	
una vaca	*one cow*	cincuenta y **una** moscas	
		*Fifty-**one** flies*	

¿Cuántas plumas tienes? Tengo **una.**	*How many pens do you have?* *I have **one**.*
Cuarenta y nueve más dos son cincuenta y **uno.**	*Forty-nine plus two equals fifty-**one**.*

Both **cien** and **ciento** mean *a hundred* or *one hundred*. Neither is preceded by **un,** and neither is followed by **y. Cien** is used only before nouns and before **mil** and **millones.**

cien trenes	*one hundred trains*
ciento treinta y siete	*one hundred thirty-seven*
cien mil habitantes	*one hundred thousand inhabitants*
ciento cuarenta y ocho mil coches	*one hundred forty-eight thousand cars*

200	doscientos	800	ochocientos
300	trescientos	900	novecientos
400	cuatrocientos	1.000	mil
500	quinientos	2.000	dos mil
600	seiscientos	1.000.000	un millón (de)
700	setecientos	2.000.000	dos millones (de)

The hundreds (**doscientos, trescientos,** etc.) also have feminine forms (**doscientas, trescientas,** etc.) and agree in gender with the noun they modify. They are not followed by **y.**

setecientas una cadenas	*701 chains*

Mil (*thousand*) is not preceded by **un** and generally is not pluralized. **Millón** (*million*) is preceded by **un,** is pluralized, and is followed by **de** when used with a noun.

mil hombres	*a thousand men*
dos mil mujeres	*two thousand women*
un millón de hombres	*one million men*
dos millones de mujeres	*two million women*

In most of the Spanish-speaking world, the comma and period are used with numbers in opposite fashion than in the United States and Canada.

2.000.000	*2,000,000*
$1.550,45	*$1,550.45*

-CER *AND* -CIR *VERBS*

All verbs that end in a vowel + **-cer** or **-cir** (except **decir** *[to say, tell]*, **hacer** *[to do, make]*, **mecer** *[to rock]*, and **cocer** *[to cook]*) have **-zc-** in the **yo** form of the present indicative, in all forms of the present subjunctive, and in **usted** and **ustedes** commands as well as in the negative **tú** commands.

OFRECER *(TO OFFER)*

Irregular Forms
Present Indicative: **ofrezco**
Present Subjunctive: **ofrezca, ofrezcas, ofrezca, ofrezcamos, ofrezcáis, ofrezcan**
Commands: **ofrezca** Ud., **ofrezcan** Uds., no **ofrezcas** tú

Other common **-cer** and **-cir** verbs include **aparecer** *(to appear)*, **merecer** *(to deserve)*, **nacer** *(to be born)*, **pertenecer** *(to belong)*, and **reconocer** *(to recognize)*.

Verbs that end in a consonant + **-cer** or **-cir** change the **-c-** to **-z-** in the **yo** form of the present indicative, in all forms of the present subjunctive, and in **usted** and **ustedes** commands as well as in negative **tú** commands. **Mecer** *(to rock)* is also included in this group.

VENCER *(TO DEFEAT)*

Irregular Forms
Present Indicative: **venzo**
Present Subjunctive: **venza, venzas, venza, venzamos, venzáis, venzan**
Commands: **venza** Ud., **venzan** Uds., no **venzas** tú

Other consonant + **-cer** or **-cir** verbs include **convencer** *(to convince)*, **ejercer** *(to exercise)*, **esparcir** *(to scatter)*, **fruncir** *(to frown)*, **uncir** *(to yoke)*, and **zurcir** *(to mend)*.
See -DUCIR *VERBS*.

CIEN(TO): *See CARDINAL NUMBERS.*

CIERTO(A) *(CERTAIN)*

Cierto(a) is not preceded by **un** or **una.**

Cierto hombre me lo dijo.	*A **certain** man told me.*
Buscaba **cierta** revista.	*I was looking for **a certain** magazine.*

COGNATES

Cognates are words that have similar or identical forms and meanings in Spanish and English.

idea	*idea*
posible	*possible*
teléfono	*telephone*

False cognates, however, have similar or identical forms but different meanings.

Common False Cognates

actual	*current, present-day*	gracioso	*funny*
asistir	*to attend*	grosería	*vulgarity*
atender	*to take care of*	ignorar	*to be a unaware of*
campo	*country*	injuria	*damage, injustice*
carta	*letter*	jubilación	*retirement*
cimiento	*foundation*	largo	*long*
conferencia	*lecture*	lectura	*reading*
decepción	*disappointment*		*(material)*
delito	*crime*	marca	*brand (name)*
desgracia	*misfortune*	marco	*frame*
editor	*publisher*	molestar	*to bother*
embarazada	*pregnant*	once	*eleven*
éxito	*success*	oración	*prayer, sentence*
fábrica	*factory*		*(grammatical)*
facultad	*college (of a university)*	pan	*bread*

pariente	*relative (family)*	restar	*subtract*
quitar	*to take away*	sano	*healthy*
realizar	*to attain, achieve*	sentencia	*verdict, sentence*
recolección	*summary*		*(legal)*
red	*net*	simpático	*nice*
		suceso	*event*

COMENZAR *(TO BEGIN, START)*

For conjugation, *see STEM-CHANGING VERBS: -AR AND -ER and -ZAR VERBS.*

COMMANDS (IMPERATIVES)

In English, commands are used when the subject *you* is understood but not expressed: *Sit down, Bring it to me, Don't go, Don't tell them,* and so on. In Spanish, commands may be in the **usted** or **ustedes** forms (formal) or in the **tú** or **vosotros** forms (familiar).

usted and ustedes Commands

Usted and **ustedes** use present subjunctive forms. In general, the **usted** command is formed by changing the **-o** of the present indicative **yo** form (**yo traigo** *I bring,* **yo como** *I eat,* **yo hablo** *I speak,* **yo cierro** *I close*) to **-a** for **-er** and **-ir** verbs and to **-e** for **-ar** verbs.

traer *to bring*	traigo *I bring*	**Traiga** (Ud.). *Bring.*
comer *to eat*	como *I eat*	**Coma** (Ud.). *Eat.*
hablar *to speak*	hablo *I speak*	**Hable** (Ud.). *Speak.*
cerrar *to close*	cierro *I close*	No **cierre** (Ud.). *Don't close.*
volver *to return*	vuelvo *I return*	No **vuelva** (Ud.). *Don't return.*

The **Uds.** commands simply add **-n** to the **Ud.** command: **traigan (Uds.)** *bring,* **coman (Uds.)** *eat,* **hablen (Uds.)** *speak,* and so on. The use of the subject pronouns **Ud.** and **Uds.** is optional.

-car, -gar, and **-zar** verbs end in **-que(n), -gue(n),** and **-ce(n)** in the **Ud.** and **Uds.** commands.

buscar	*to look for*	**Busque** el dinero.	***Look for*** *the money.*
pagar	*to pay*	**Pague** la cuenta.	***Pay*** *the bill.*
cruzar	*to cross*	No **crucen** aquí.	*Don't **cross** here.*

The following five verbs have irregular **Ud.** and **Uds.** commands:

ir	*to go*	**Vaya(n).**	***Go.***
ser	*to be*	**Sea(n).**	***Be.***
saber	*to know*	**Sepa(n).**	***Know.***
dar	*to give*	**Dé, den.**	***Give.***
estar	*to be*	**Esté(n).**	***Be.***

Ud. and **Uds.** commands of reflexive verbs are formed in the same manner as other verbs except **-se** is attached to an affirmative command and is placed before a negative command.

levantarse	*to get up*	**Levántese.** *Get up.*	No **se levante.** *Don't **get up.***
vestirse	*to get dressed*	**Vístanse.** *Get dressed.*	No **se vistan.** *Don't **get dressed.***

tú Commands

In general, the affirmative **tú** command is the same as the third person, or **él,** form of the present indicative. The use of the personal pronoun **tú** is optional.

El come.	*He eats.*	**Come** (tú).	***Eat.***
El estudia.	*He studies.*	**Estudia** (tú).	***Study.***
El piensa.	*He thinks.*	**Piensa** (tú).	***Think.***
El duerme.	*He sleeps.*	**Duerme** (tú).	***Sleep.***

The following are the most common irregular affirmative **tú** commands:

decir	*to say, tell*	**Di** (tú).	*Say. Tell.*
hacer	*to make, do*	**Haz** (tú).	*Make. Do.*
ir	*to go*	**Ve** (tú).	*Go.*
poner	*to put*	**Pon** (tú).	*Put.*
salir	*to leave*	**Sal** (tú).	*Leave.*
ser	*to be*	**Sé** (tú).	*Be.*
tener	*to have*	**Ten** (tú).	*Have.*
venir	*to come*	**Ven** (tú).	*Come.*

All negative **tú** commands are formed by adding **-s** to the **usted** command.

hablar	*to speak*	No **hables** (tú).	*Don't speak.*
volver	*to return*	No **vuelvas** (tú).	*Don't return.*
ir	*to go*	No **vayas** (tú).	*Don't go.*
salir	*to leave*	No **salgas** (tú).	*Don't leave.*

Tú commands of reflexive verbs are formed the same way as with other verbs except that **-te** is attached to the affirmative forms and is placed before the negative forms.

acostarse *to go to bed*	**Acuéstate** (tú). *Go to bed.*	**No te acuestes.** *Don't go to bed.*
vestirse *to get dressed*	**Vístete** (tú). *Get dressed.*	**No te vistas** (tú). *Don't get dressed.*

vosotros Commands

The affirmative **vosotros** command is formed by changing the final **-r** of the infinitive to **-d.** Reflexive verbs (except **irse**) drop the **-d** of the command and add the reflexive pronoun **-os.** Reflexive **-ir** verbs require the addition of a written accent to the final **i.**

comer	**Comed** con nosotros.	*Eat with us.*
decir	**Decid** la verdad.	*Tell the truth.*
sentarse	**Sentaos** aquí.	*Sit here.*
vestirse	**Vestíos** pronto.	*Get dressed quickly.*
irse	**Idos** de aquí.	*Go away from here.*

The negative **vosotros** commands are the same as the **vosotros** form of the present subjunctive.

comer	No **comáis** aquí.	*Don't eat here.*
decir	No **digáis** mentiras.	*Don't tell lies.*
sentarse	No **os sentéis** aquí.	*Don't sit here.*
irse	No **os vayáis** todavía.	*Don't leave yet.*

See INDIRECT COMMANDS, LET'S, and PRESENT TENSE SUBJUNCTIVE.
All object pronouns and reflexive pronouns are attached to affirmative commands and precede negative commands.

Dí**melo.**	*Tell it to me.*
No **me lo** digas.	*Don't tell it to me.*
Escríba**les.**	*Write to them.*
No **les** escriba.	*Don't write to them.*
Levánte**nse.**	*Get up.*
No **se** levanten.	*Don't get up.*

CÓMO: *See INTERROGATIVES.*

COMO SI *(AS IF)*

Como si is always followed by either the imperfect subjunctive or the past perfect subjunctive.

Me mira **como si** me **conociera.**	*He's looking at me **as if** he **knew** me.*
Lo comió **como si** le **hubiera gustado.**	*He ate it **as if** he **had liked** it.*

COMPARATIVES

Comparisons of Equality: *See AS . . . AS* (TAN . . . COMO) *and AS MUCH/MANY AS* (TANTO[S] COMO).

Comparisons of Inequality

In English, the comparative form is generally either *-er* (*bigger, taller, funnier*) or *more/less* (*more* interesting, *more* exciting, *less* complicated). In Spanish, the comparative is usually formed with **más** or **menos.** *Than* is expressed by **que** except before numbers, where it is translated by **de.**

Mi casa es **más grande que** tu casa.	*My house is **larger than** your house.*
El fútbol es **más interesante que** el béisbol.	*Football is **more interesting than** baseball.*
Es **menos** común.	*It is **less** common.*
Tiene **más de** veinte.	*He has **more than** twenty.*

The following adjectives have irregular comparative forms:

bueno	*good*	mejor	*better*
malo	*bad*	peor	*worse*
viejo	*old*	mayor	*older—for people*
joven	*young*	menor	*younger*
mucho	*much, many*	más	*more*
poco	*little, few*	menos	*less, fewer*

Pelé era **mejor** jugador que Bebeto.	*Pelé was a **better** player than Bebeto.*
Esa revista es **peor** que la otra.	*That magazine is **worse** than the other one.*
Yo soy **mayor** que mi hermana.	*I am **older** than my sister.*
Mi hermana es **menor** que yo.	*My sister is **younger** than I.*

See SUPERLATIVES and THAN.

Adverbs are compared in the same way as adjectives. The following adverbs have irregular comparative forms:

mucho	*a lot, very*	más	*more*
poco	*little*	menos	*less*
bien	*well*	mejor	*better*
mal	*badly*	peor	*worse*

COMPOUND TENSES

In English, a *compound tense* is a verbal expression consisting of two parts that may be either a form of the verb *to be* + a present participle (*they are eating, he was working*) or a form of the verb *to have* + a past participle (*she has left, they will have returned*). In Spanish, these correspond to a form of **estar** + present participle (**están comiendo, estaba trabajando**) and a form of **haber** + past participle (**ha salido, habrán vuelto**). *See PERFECT TENSES,* HABER, *PAST PARTICIPLE, and PRESENT PARTICIPLE.*

CON TAL DE QUE (PROVIDED THAT)

Con tal de que is always followed by a verb in the subjunctive mood.

Voy con él **con tal de que** él **pague.**	*I'll go with him **provided that** he pays.*

See PRESENT TENSE SUBJUNCTIVE.

CONDITIONAL PERFECT TENSE

The *conditional perfect tense* consists of the conditional tense of **haber** + a past participle. It usually translates *would have* + a past participle and is frequently used with the past perfect subjunctive. Pronoun objects must precede the auxiliary verb.

Yo le **habría dicho.**	*I **would have** told him.*
Tú **habrías salido.**	*You **would have** left.*
Él, ella, Ud. **habría pagado.**	*He, she, you **would have** paid.*
Nosotros lo **habríamos comprado.**	*We **would have** bought it.*

Vosotros **habríais muerto.**	*You **would have** died.*
Ellos, Uds. me **habrían visto.**	*They, you **would have** seen me.*
Yo **habría ido** si me hubieran invitado.	*I **would have gone** if they had invited me.*

The conditional perfect tense is also used to express probability or speculation about the past.

Habrían estado en casa.	*They **had probably** been home.*
¿Lo **habría hecho** él?	*I **wonder** if he **had done** it.*

CONDITIONAL TENSE

All verbs in Spanish have the same endings in the conditional tense. Most verbs add the following endings to the infinitive: **ía, ías, ía, íamos, íais, ían.**

HABLAR *(TO SPEAK, TALK)*

yo	hablar**ía**	nosotros	hablar**íamos**
tú	hablar**ías**	vosotros	hablar**íais**
él, ella, Ud.	hablar**ía**	ellos, Uds.	hablar**ían**

The following are the most common irregular verbs in the conditional tense. They use the same endings as regular verbs but attach them to special stems and not to the infinitive:

Infinitive		**Stem**	
caber	*(to fit)*	**cabr-**	cabría, cabrías, etc.
decir	*(to say, tell)*	**dir-**	diría, dirías, etc.
haber	*(to have)*	**habr-**	habría, habrías, etc.
hacer	*(to make, do)*	**har-**	haría, harías, etc.
poder	*(to be able to)*	**podr-**	podría, podrías, etc.
poner	*(to put)*	**pondr-**	pondría, pondrías, etc.
querer	*(to want)*	**querr-**	querría, querrías, etc.
saber	*(to know)*	**sabr-**	sabría, sabrías, etc.
salir	*(to leave)*	**saldr-**	saldría, saldrías, etc.
tener	*(to have)*	**tendr-**	tendría, tendrías, etc.
valer	*(to be worth)*	**valdr-**	valdría, valdrías, etc.
venir	*(to come)*	**vendr-**	vendría, vendrías, etc.

The conditional tense translates *would* or *wouldn't*. It is frequently used with the imperfect subjunctive.

No **hablaría** con él.	*I **wouldn't** talk with him.*
Yo te **diría.**	*I **would** tell you.*
Compraría un boleto si **tuviera** el dinero.	*I **would** buy a ticket if I had the money.*

The conditional tense is also used to express probability or speculation about the past. In a question, it may translate *I wonder.*

Trabajarían toda la mañana.	*They **probably** worked all morning.*
¿Cuándo **regresaría** ella?	*I **wonder** when she returned.*

The imperfect tense indicative, not the conditional tense, translates **would** when describing a repeated or habitual action in the past. Compare the following examples.

Yo visitaba a mi abuela cada noche cuando vivíamos en Denver.	*I **would visit** my grandmother every night when we lived in Denver.*
Yo visitaría a mi abuela esta noche si viviéramos en Denver.	*I **would visit** my grandmother tonight if we lived in Denver.*

CONJUGATE

To *conjugate* means to change a verb from the infinitive form (**ver, salir,** etc.) to its personal forms in the various tenses and moods. For example, **ver** is conjugated in the present tense indicative as follows: **Yo veo, tú ves, él ve, nosotros vemos, vosotros veis, ellos ven.** *See INFINITIVE.*

CONJUNCTIONS

Coordinating conjunctions (and, but, or, either . . . or, neither . . . nor) join words, phrases, or clauses of equal value. See *AND:* Y *VS.* E, *BUT:* PERO *VS.* SINO, *OR:* O *VS.* U, *and AFFIRMATIVE AND NEGATIVE INDEFINITES.*

Subordinating conjunctions join subordinate (dependent) clauses to main clauses. The following are commonly used subordinate conjunctions:

a fin de que	*so that, in order that*	donde	*where*
a menos que	*unless*	en caso (de) que	*in case*
antes (de) que	*before*	hasta que	*until*
aunque	*although, even though*	mientras (que)	*while*
como	*as, since*	para que	*so that, in order*
como si	*as if*		*that*
con tal (de) que	*provided that*	porque	*because*
cuando	*when*	puesto que	*since*
de modo que	*so, so that*	que	*that*
desde que	*since*	si	*if, whether*
después (de) que	*after*	sin que	*without*

See *PRESENT TENSE SUBJUNCTIVE.*

CONMIGO

With me is always translated as **conmigo** and never as **con mí.**

No quería ir **conmigo.**	*She didn't want to go **with me.***

See *PREPOSITIONAL PRONOUNS.*

CONOCER *(TO KNOW)*

For conjugation, *see* -CER *AND* -CIR *VERBS.*
Conocer means *knew* in the imperfect tense and *met* in the preterit tense.

Yo la **conocía** cuando vivía en Las Cruces.	*I **knew** her when I lived in Las Cruces.*
Yo la **conocí** en Lordsburg.	*I **met** her in Lordsburg.*

CONOCER *VS.* SABER: See *KNOW:* SABER *VS.* CONOCER.

CONSONANTS: See *A Note on Pronunciation, p. 3.*

CONSIGO: See *REFLEXIVE PRONOUNS.*

CONTIGO

Contigo, not **con ti,** expresses *with you.*

¿Salió **contigo?**	*Did he go out **with you?***

See PREPOSITIONAL PRONOUNS.

CONTRACTIONS: See AL (A + EL) *and* DEL (DE + EL).

COULD: See PODER.

COUNTRY: PAÍS (NACIÓN) *VS.* CAMPO

Country in the sense of *nation* is **país** or **nación;** *countryside* is **campo.**

La Argentina es el **país** más grande de habla española.	*Argentina is the largest Spanish-speaking **country.***
Prefiero vivir en el **campo;** no me gusta la ciudad.	*I prefer to live in the **country;** I don't like the city.*

CREER *(TO BELIEVE)*

For conjugation, *see -EER VERBS.*

CUÁL *VS.* QUÉ

Qué translates *what* and is used in requesting a definition.

¿**Qué** es una diéresis?	*What is a dieresis?*

Cuál may translate *what, which,* or *which one,* and is used in the context of selection.

¿**Cuál** es más barato?	*Which one is cheaper?*

Qué is often used before nouns. **Cuál** is not normally used before nouns.

¿**Qué** cinta prefieres?	*What tape do you prefer?*
¿**Cuál** es la cinta que prefieres?	*Which is the tape that you prefer?*

Cuáles is the plural of **cuál** and translates *which* or *which ones.*

¿**Cuáles** son los mejores?	***Which (ones) are the best?***

See INTERROGATIVES and RELATIVE PRONOUNS.

CUALQUIER(A)

Cualquier(a) and its plural **cualesquier(a)** mean *any* in the sense of *all* or *every* as well as *whatever, whichever,* and *whomever.* Before a singular noun, the apocopated form **cualquier** is normally used. **Cualquiera** must be used when the noun is not expressed. **Cualquier(a)** should not be confused with **ninguno,** which means *any* in the sense of *none* or *not any.*

Cualquier mecánico puede arreglar tu carro.	***Any*** *mechanic can fix your car.*
¿Qué video quieres alquilar? **Cualquiera.**	*What video do you want to rent?* ***Any one (whichever).***
Mi primo saldrá con **cualquier** chica que lleve una falda corta.	*My cousin will go out with **any** girl who wears a short skirt.*
Mi primo no saldrá con **ninguna** chica que lleve una falda corta.	*My cousin won't go out with **any** girl who wears a short skirt.*

See ANY.

CUÁNTO(A): *See INTERROGATIVES.*

CUBIERTO

Past participle of **cubrir** *(to cover).*

CUYO: *See RELATIVE PRONOUNS and WHOSE: CUYO VS. ¿DE QUIÉN(ES)?*

D

DAR *(TO GIVE)*

Irregular Forms
Present Indicative: **doy**
Preterit: **di, diste, dio, dimos, disteis, dieron**
Present Subjunctive: **dé, des, dé, demos, deis, den**
Imperfect Subjunctive: **diera, dieras,** etc.; **diese, dieses,** etc.

Idiomatic Expressions with *dar*

dar a *to face*
dar a conocer *to make known*
dar brincos (saltos) *to jump*
dar con *to find*
dar cuerda *to wind (clock, toy, etc.)*
dar de alta *to discharge a patient*
dar de baja *to discharge a soldier*
dar de beber (tomar) *to give to drink*
dar de comer *to feed*
dar el pésame *to express condolences*
dar en *to hit, strike*
dar(le) ganas de *to feel like*
dar gusto *to please*
dar la mano *to shake hands*
dar las espaldas *to turn one's back on*
dar las gracias *to thank*

dar lata *to pester, cause trouble*
dar por *to consider*
dar prestado *to lend*
dar que hacer *to cause trouble*
dar un abrazo *to hug*
dar un paseo *to take a walk*
dar un vistazo *to glance*
darse a conocer *to make oneself* dar
  known
darse cuenta de *to realize*
dárselas de *to pose as, brag about*
darse por *to consider oneself*
darse por vencido *to give up,*
  surrender
darse vuelta *to turn*

DATES

¿Cuál es la **fecha** (de) hoy?	*What's the **date** today?*
¿Qué **fecha** es hoy?	*What's **the date** today?*
¿A cuántos estamos?	*What's the date today?*

The formula for giving the date is **el** + day + **de** + month + **de** + year.

El siete **de** mayo **de** mil novecientos noventa y cinco.	*May 7, 1995*
El cuatro **de** julio **de** mil setecientos setenta y seis.	*July 4, 1776*
El primero de enero **de** mil novecientos ochenta y nueve.	*January 1, 1989*

Cardinal numbers are used for all dates except the first, which uses **primero**.

DAYS OF THE WEEK

el lunes	*Monday*
el martes	*Tuesday*
el miércoles	*Wednesday*
el jueves	*Thursday*
el viernes	*Friday*
el sábado	*Saturday*
el domingo	*Sunday*

The days of the week are not capitalized in Spanish. **El viernes** is either *Friday* or *on Friday*. **El** or **los** is always used with days of the week unless one is using a form of **ser** to tell what day of the week it is. The preposition *en (on)* is not used with days of the week.

Hoy **es lunes** y ayer **fue domingo.**	*Today **is Monday** and yesterday **was Sunday.***
No trabajo **los domingos.**	*I don't work **on Sundays.***
Llegamos **el martes.**	*We arrive **on Tuesday.***
La fiesta es **el sábado.**	*The party is **on Saturday.***

DE (SPECIAL USES)

De *(of, from)* is used in several important grammatical constructions.

1. Substitute for apostrophe denoting possession

There is no apostrophe in Spanish. A phrase with **de** substitutes for the apostrophe.

las patas **de** la mesa	*the table's legs (the legs **of** the table)*
la falda **de** Rosa	*Rosa's skirt (the skirt **of** Rosa)*
el reloj **del** abogado	*the lawyer's watch (the watch **of** the lawyer)*

2. To translate *in*

After a superlative, **de,** not **en,** translates *in.*

el hombre más fuerte **de** Texas	*the strongest man **in** Texas*
Elena es la chica más alta **de** la clase.	*Elena is the tallest girl **in** the class.*

3. To translate *than*

Before a number or a relative pronoun, **de** translates *than.*

Emilio tiene más **de** veinte éxitos.	*Emilio has more **than** twenty hits.*
Carmen puede tomar más cervezas **de** las que él compró.	*Carmen can drink more beer **than** he bought.*

Más que is translated as *only* before a number in a negative sentence.

Emilio no tiene **más que** veinte dólares.	*Emilio has **only** twenty dollars.*

4. To translate *whose* in questions

¿**De quién** es la chamarra?	***Whose** jacket is it?*
¿**De quién** son los cuadros?	***Whose** paintings are they?*

See WHOSE: CUYO *VS.* ¿DE QUIÉN(ES)?

5. To ask what color something is

¿**De qué color** es la camisa?	*What color is the shirt?*

6. To ask or tell what something is made (out) of

¿**De qué es** el juguete? **Es de** plástico.	*What is the toy made of? It's made out of plastic.*

See POSSESSION WITH DE *and PREPOSITIONS.*

DE + EL: *See* DEL: DE + EL.

DEBER (DE)

Deber means *should* or *ought to* and is followed by an infinitive. Sometimes the conditional (**debería, deberías,** etc.) or the imperfect subjunctive (**debiera, debieras,** etc.) substitutes for the present tense. **Deber** also means *to owe.*

Debes estudiar más.	*You ought to study more.*
Ella **debiera dejar**lo.	*She should leave him.*
Debemos decirle mañana.	*We should tell her tomorrow.*
No te **debo** nada.	*I don't owe you anything.*

Deber de means *must* in the sense of *probably* and is followed by an infinitive.

Tú **debes de estudiar** mucho.	*You probably study a lot.*
Debe de estar enfermo.	*He must be sick.*

DECIR (TO SAY, TELL)

Irregular Forms
Present Indicative: **digo, dices, dice,** decimos, decís, **dicen**
Preterit: **dije, dijiste, dijo, dijimos, dijisteis, dijeron**
Future: **diré, dirás,** etc.
Conditional: **diría, dirías,** etc.
Present Subjunctive: **diga, digas, diga, digamos, digáis, digan**

Imperfect Subjunctive: **dijera,** etc.; **dijese,** etc.
Present Participle: **diciendo**
Past Participle: **dicho**
Imperative: **di** (tú)

DEFINITE ARTICLES

The English definite article *the* has four equivalents in Spanish (**el, la, los, las**), and each represents a specific gender and number: masculine singular **el lago,** *the lake;* feminine singular **la moneda,** *the coin;* masculine plural **los lagos,** *the lakes;* and feminine plural **las monedas,** *the coins.* For a discussion of gender, *see NOUNS.*

The Spanish definite articles are sometimes used in situations where the English definite article is omitted.

The following are some special uses of definite articles.

1. With days of the week

Hay una fiesta **el sábado.**	*There is a party (**on**) **Saturday.***
¿Estudias **los viernes?**	*Do you study (**on**) **Fridays?***

The definite article is omitted after forms of **ser** when indicating what day of the week it is.

Hoy **es martes.**	*Today **is Tuesday.***

2. With titles

La señora López ganó el premio.	***Mrs. López*** *won the prize.*
El presidente Lincoln fue el mejor.	***President Lincoln*** *was the best.*
La profesora Méndez me dijo ayer.	***Professor Méndez*** *told me yesterday.*

In direct discourse, the definite article is omitted before a title.

¿Cómo está usted, **profesora Méndez?**	*How are you, **Professor Méndez?***

3. With the seasons of the year

La primavera es muy bonita.	*Spring is very pretty.*
No me gusta **el invierno.**	*I don't like **winter.***

After forms of **ser** and the prepositions **de** and **en,** the article may be omitted before a season.

Nos conocimos un día **de verano.**	*We met on a **summer** day.*

4. With meals

Sirven **el desayuno** muy temprano.	*They serve **breakfast** very early.*

5. With nouns used in a general sense, abstract nouns, and academic disciplines

Los caballos son animales fuertes.	*Horses are strong animals.*
El amor es bello.	*Love is beautiful.*
La física es muy importante.	*Physics is very important.*

6. With infinitives used as subjects

El fumar está prohibido.	*Smoking is prohibited.*

7. With weights and measures

Cobran veinte dólares **la onza.**	*They charge twenty dollars **an (per) ounce.***
La gasolina cuesta más de seis pesos **el litro.**	*Gas costs more than six pesos **a (per) liter.***

8. With proper nouns modified by adjectives

la bella España	*beautiful Spain*

9. With certain countries, states, and cities

la Argentina	*Argentina*
el Brasil	*Brazil*
el Canadá	*Canada*
el Cairo	*Cairo*
el Cuzco	*Cuzco*
el Ecuador	*Ecuador*
los Estados Unidos	*the United States*
la Florida	*Florida*
la Habana	*Havana*
la India	*India*
el Japón	*Japan*
el Paraguay	*Paraguay*
el Perú	*Peru*
la República Dominicana	*the Dominican Republic*
El Salvador	*El Salvador*
el Uruguay	*Uruguay*

10. In place of the possessive referring to parts of the body and articles of clothing when the possessor's identity is obvious

Me lastimé **el dedo.**	*I hurt **my finger.***
Se puso **los pantalones.**	*He put on **his pants.***
¿Te quitaste **los zapatos**?	*Did you take off **your shoes**?*

When the identity of the possessor is not obvious, the possessive adjective is used with parts of the body and articles of clothing.

Yo llevaba **su vestido.**	*I was wearing **her dress.***
Mi camisa está en el ropero.	***My shirt** is in the closet.*

11. With languages

El español no es difícil.	***Spanish** isn't difficult.*
Me gusta **el italiano.**	*I like **Italian.***

The definite article **el** is not normally used with languages after the verb **hablar** or after the prepositions **de** and **en.** It is usually omitted after forms of **aprender, estudiar,** and other verbs commonly used with languages.

Me habló **en japonés.**	*He spoke to me **in Japanese.***
¿**Hablas ruso?**	***Do you speak Russian?***

With an intervening adverb between the verb and the language, **el** is required.

Hablas muy bien **el** ruso.	*You speak Russian very well.*

12. With the time of day

Son **las ocho.**	*It's **eight o'clock.***
Comí a **la una.**	*I ate at **one o'clock.***

13. With sports and games

El básquetbol es muy rápido.	***Basketball** is very fast.*

See LO.

DEJAR (DE)

Dejar + infinitive means *to allow, let,* or *permit.* **Dejar de** + infinitive means *to stop doing (something).*

Su papá no la **deja salir** con él.	*Her father **doesn't allow** her **to go out** with him.*
No me **dejaron fumar.**	*They **didn't let** me **smoke.***
Mi tío **dejó de fumar** hace cinco años.	*My uncle **stopped smoking** five years ago.*

See LEAVE: DEJAR *VS.* SALIR.

DEL (DE + EL)

De *(from, of)* + **el** *(the)* must contract to **del.**

Viene **del** hospital.	*She's coming **from the** hospital.*
No me gustó la portada **del** libro.	*I didn't like **the** book's cover.*

However, **de** *(from, of)* + **él** *(him)* does not contract.

El coche **de él** es azul.	*His car is blue.*

DEMONSTRATIVE ADJECTIVES AND PRONOUNS

este juego	ese juego	aquel juego
this game	*that game*	*that game*
esta oficina	esa oficina	aquella oficina
this office	*that office*	*that office*
estos juegos	esos juegos	aquellos juegos
these games	*those games*	*those games*
estas oficinas	esas oficinas	aquellas oficinas
these offices	*those offices*	*those offices*

Demonstrative adjectives generally precede the noun they modify. When a demonstrative adjective follows the noun it modifies, a definite article precedes the noun.

Salió con **ese tipo.**	*She went out with **that guy.***
Salió con **el tipo ese.**	*She went out with **that guy.***

The difference between **ese, esa,** etc., and **aquel, aquella,** etc. is one of relative distance, with the **aquel/aquella** forms being at a greater distance from the speaker. As adjectives, these forms do not have accent marks, but when they are used as pronouns, they have an accent mark over the first **e.** The singular pronoun forms (**éste/ésta** and **ése/ésa, aquél/aquélla**) translate as *this one* and *that one,* respectively. Like other adjectives and pronouns, the demonstratives must agree in number and gender with the nouns they modify or replace.

Charro tiene clases en **este salón** y Norma tiene clases en **ése.**	*Charro has classes in **this** classroom, and Norma has classes in **that one.***
Me hospedé en **aquel hotel** y Ana se hospedó en **éste.**	*I stayed in **that** hotel, and Ana stayed in **this one.***

Carlos nunca trabajó en **esta fábrica** y no trabajó en **aquélla** tampoco.	*Carlos never worked in **this factory**, and he didn't work in **that one** either.*

Me gustan **estas cortinas,** pero no me gustan **ésas.**	*I like **these curtains**, but I don't like **those**.*

In Spanish, *the latter* (**éste, ésta, éstos, éstas**) and *the former* (**aquél, aquélla, aquéllos, aquéllas**) appear in reverse order than in English.

Esmeralda y Carlos son primos. **Éste** es ingeniero civil y **aquélla** es ingeniera química.	*Esmeralda and Carlos are cousins. **The latter** is a civil engineer, and **the former** is a chemical engineer.*

The neuter relative pronouns are **esto** *(this),* **eso** *(that),* and **aquello** *(that)* and refer to unidentified objects or to statements or ideas that have been mentioned. They do not have accent marks.

¿Qué es **esto**?	*What is **this**?*
¿Te gustó **eso**?	*Did you like **that**?*
¿Qué es **aquello**?	*What is **that**?*

DEPENDENT CLAUSE: *See PRESENT TENSE SUBJUNCTIVE.*

DEVOLVER: *See RETURN:* VOLVER *VS.* DEVOLVER.

DICHO

Past participle of **decir** *(to say, tell).*

DIERESIS

The **u** in **gue** (**guerra,** *war*) and **gui** (**guitarra,** *guitar*) is always silent. However, the *dieresis* (two dots over the **ü,** as in **bilingüe** *bilingual,* **pingüino** *penguin*) indicates that the **u** is pronounced.

DIMINUTIVES: *See SUFFIXES.*

DIPHTHONGS

When the unaccented weak vowels **u** and **i** are next to each other or to the strong vowels (**a, e, o**), they combine to form a *diphthong*. The two vowels in a diphthong are always in the same syllable: s**ie**te, f**ue**, r**ui**do.

DIRECT OBJECT PRONOUNS

me	*me*	nos	*us*
te	*you (familiar)*	os	*you (plural familiar)*
lo, le*	*you (masculine), it (masculine), him*	los	*them, you (plural masculine)*
la	*you (feminine), it (feminine), her*	las	*them, you (plural feminine)*

*****le** is sometimes used instead of **lo,** especially in Spain, to mean *him* or *you.*

Direct object pronouns come before conjugated verbs including the auxiliary verb (**haber,** *to have*).

Juan **me conoce.**	*Juan **knows me.***
No **te oigo.**	*I don't **hear you.***
Nos ven.	***They see us.***
¿Tienes el dinero? Sí, **lo tengo.**	*Do you have the money? Yes, **I have it.***
¿Tienes la escoba? Sí, **la tengo.**	*Do you have the broom? Yes, **I have it.***
¿**Me ve** Ud.? Sí, **lo veo.**	*Do you see me? Yes, I see you.*
¿La cuenta? Ya **la he pagado.**	*The bill? **I've** already **paid it.***

When a conjugated verb and a present participle or a conjugated verb and an infinitive are together, the direct object pronoun may be attached to the infinitive or the present participle, or it may come before the conjugated verb.

No puedo ayudar**te.**	*I can't help **you.***
No **te** puedo ayudar.	*I can't help **you.***
Estoy vendiéndo**los.**	*I am selling **them.***
Los estoy vendiendo.	*I am selling **them.***

When used with an infinitive, verbs like **gustar** that are normally used with an indirect object pronoun require that other object pronouns be attached to the infinitive.

¿**Te** gusta hacer**lo**?	*Do **you** like to do **it**?*
Me duele decir**te**.	*It pains **me** to tell **you**.*

Object pronouns must be attached to affirmative commands, but they must precede negative commands.

Míre**lo**.	*Look at it.*	No **lo** mire.	*Don't look at it.*
Escúcha**los**.	*Listen to them.*	No **los** escuches.	*Don't listen to them.*
Lláma**me**.	*Call me.*	No **me** llames.	*Don't call me.*

If a direct object noun precedes the verb, a redundant direct object pronoun is used in addition to the noun.

A esa **muchacha** no **la** conozco.	*I don't know that **girl**.*
Estos **libros** no **los** tengo.	*I don't have these **books**.*

DIVISION OF WORDS INTO SYLLABLES (SYLLABIFICATION)

Single consonants between vowels always go with the vowel that follows.

económico	**e-co-nó-mi-co**

Two consonants between vowels are separated unless the second of the two is an **l** or **r;** however, **l** is separated from a preceding **n,** and **r** is separated from a preceding **l** or **n.**

importante	**im-por-tan-te**
padre	**pa-dre**
Enrique	**En-ri-que**

Only the last consonant of a group of three goes with the vowel that follows unless the last one is an **l** or **r.**

inspector	**ins-pec-tor**
introducir	**in-tro-du-cir**

Combinations of unaccented **u** or **i** with each other or any other vowel form diphthongs and are in the same syllable.

cualidad	**cua-li-dad**
aceite	**a-cei-te**
viuda	**viu-da**

All other vowels occurring together, including accented **ú** and **í,** are in separate syllables.

tarea	**ta-re-a**
traía	**tra-í-a**

DOLER *(TO ACHE, PAIN, HURT)*

For conjugation, *see STEM-CHANGING -AR AND-ER VERBS.*
Doler is used much like the verb **gustar.** (*See* GUSTAR.) When **doler** is used with a part of the body, the definite article and not the possessive adjective is used before the body part.

Me duele la cabeza.	*My head hurts.*
Le duelen los pies.	*Her feet hurt.*

-DUCIR *VERBS*

All verbs that end in **-ducir** have **-zc-** in the **yo** form of the present indicative, in all forms of the present subjunctive, in **usted** and **ustedes** commands, and in the negative **tú** command.

TRADUCIR *(TO TRANSLATE)*
Irregular Forms
Present Indicative: **traduzco**
Preterit: **traduje, tradujiste, tradujo, tradujimos, tradujisteis, tradujeron**
Present Subjunctive: **traduzca, traduzcas, traduzca, traduzcamos, traduzcáis, traduzcan**
Imperfect Subjunctive: **tradujera,** etc.; **tradujese,** etc.

Other common **-ducir** verbs include **conducir** *(to drive, lead),* **introducir** *(to introduce, insert),* and **producir** *(to produce).*

See -CER AND -CIR VERBS.

E

E: *See AND:* Y VS. E.

EACH OTHER: *See REFLEXIVE PRONOUNS.*

-EER VERBS

Verbs ending in **-eer** require **-yó** and **-yeron** instead of **-ió** and **-ieron** in the third persons singular and plural, respectively, of the preterit tense. They also take a **-y-** in all forms of the imperfect subjunctive and end in **-yendo** instead of **-iendo** in the present participle.

LEER *(TO READ)*
Irregular Forms
Preterit: leí, **leíste, leyó, leímos, leísteis, leyeron**
Imperfect Subjunctive: **leyera,** etc.; **leyese,** etc.
Present Participle: **leyendo**

Other common **-eer** verbs include **creer** *(to believe),* and **poseer** *(to possess).*

-EÍR VERBS

Verbs ending in **-eír** change the **-e-** of the stem to **-i-** and use **-endo, -ó,** and **-eron** instead of **-iendo, -ió,** and **-ieron** for their present participle and third-person preterit endings. Additionally, several forms require written accents.

REÍR *(TO LAUGH)*
Irregular Forms
Present Indicative: **río, ríes, ríe, reímos, reís, ríen**
Preterit: reí, **reíste, rio, reímos, reísteis, rieron**

Present Subjunctive: **ría, rías, ría, riamos, riáis, rían**
Imperfect Subjunctive: **riera, rieras,** etc.; **riese, rieses,** etc.
Imperative: **ríe**
Present Participle: **riendo**
Past Participle: **reído**

Other common **-eír** verbs include **engreírse** *(to become conceited),* **freír** *(to fry),* and **sonreír** *(to smile).*

EL: *See DEFINITE ARTICLES.*

ÉL: *See PREPOSITIONAL PRONOUNS and SUBJECT PRONOUNS.*

ELISION

Elision is the omission of a vowel, consonant, or syllable in pronunciation. In Spanish, this usually takes the form of the omission of a vowel when one word ends and the next one begins with that same vowel.

Él **ha a**bierto la puerta.

ELLA (ELLAS, ELLOS):

See PREPOSITIONAL PRONOUNS and SUBJECT PRONOUNS.

ELLO

Ello is occasionally used as an object of a preposition or a subject pronoun to mean **it** in reference to a situation or condition that has been previously mentioned. It never refers to a specific noun. **Ello** is uncommon in contemporary Spanish, having been replaced by **eso.**

Hablaré de **ello** la próxima vez.	*I will talk about **it** next time.*
Hablaré de **eso** la próxima vez.	*I will talk about **it** next time.*
Tuvo que tomar el autobús y **ello** (**eso**) resultó una pérdida de tiempo.	*He had to take the bus and **it** turned out to be a waste of time.*

See DEMONSTRATIVE ADJECTIVES AND PRONOUNS, PREPOSITIONAL PRONOUNS, and SUBJECT PRONOUNS.

EMPEZAR *(TO BEGIN, START)*

For conjugation, see *STEM-CHANGING VERBS: -AR AND -ER and -ZAR VERBS.*

EN

En commonly translates the English **in, at,** and **on.**
See PREPOSITIONS.

-ERÍA: *See SUFFIXES.*

ESE (ESA, ESO, ESAS, ESOS): *See DEMON-STRATIVE ADJECTIVES AND PRONOUNS.*

ESCRIBIR *(TO WRITE)*

Irregular Form
Past Participle: **escrito**

ESDRÚJULA (PALABRA)

A **palabra esdrújula** is a word whose stress is on the antepenult (third from the end) syllable (est**ó**mago, m**é**dico, (d**á**melas).
See ACCENT MARK.

ESPERAR *(TO HOPE, WAIT FOR, EXPECT)*

When esperar means to wait for, neither **por** nor **para** is needed to express *for.*

Espero el autobus en la esquina.   *I wait for the bus on the corner.*

ESTE (ESTA, ESTO, ESTAS, ESTOS): *See DEMONSTRATIVE ADJECTIVES AND PRONOUNS.*

ESTAR *(TO BE)*

Irregular Forms
Present Indicative: **estoy, estás, está,** estamos, estáis, **están**
Preterit: **estuve, estuviste, estuvo, estuvimos, estuvisteis, estuvieron**

Present Subjunctive: **esté, estés, esté, estemos, estéis, estén**
Imperfect Subjunctive: **estuviera,** etc.; **estuviese,** etc.
Imperative: **está** (tú)

ESTAR *VS.* SER: *See* SER *VS.* ESTAR.

ESCRITO

Past participle of **escribir** *(to write).*

EXCLAMATION MARKS: *See PUNCTUATION.*

F

FAMILIAR (TÚ, VOSOTROS) VS. FORMAL (UD., UDS.): *See SUBJECT PRONOUNS.*

FEMININE WORDS: *See DEFINITE ARTICLES, INDEFINITE ARTICLES, and NOUNS.*

FOR: See POR *VS.* PARA.

FORMAL (UD., UDS.) VS. FAMILIAR (TÚ, VOSOTROS): *See SUBJECT PRONOUNS.*

FORMER: *See DEMONSTRATIVE ADJECTIVES AND PRONOUNS.*

FRACTIONS (FRACCIONES/QUEBRADOS)

The denominator of a fraction is rendered by *ordinal numbers* from **cuarto** *(fourth)* through **décimo** *(tenth)*. Beginning with **onzavo** *(eleventh)*, the denominator is normally derived by adding **-avo** to the cardinal number. Except for numbers ending in **-siete** or **-nueve**, the final vowel of the cardinal number is dropped before adding **-avo**. The plural (**-avos**) is appended if the numerator is greater than one. **Medio** and **tercio** are used for *half* and *third*, respectively. Spanish uses *cardinal numbers* for the numerator of a fraction.

un medio *one-half*
un tercio *one-third*
dos quintos *two-fifths*

tres octavos *three-eighths*
siete onzavos *seven-elevenths*
cinco diecisieteavos *five-seventeenths*

un veintavo *one-twentieth*
seis veintinueveavos
  six twenty-ninths
once cincuentavos *eleven-fiftieths*

un setentavo *one-seventieth*
cinco centavos *five-hundredths*
un milésimo *one-thousandth*

Note that **centavo(s)** *(hundredth[s])* drops the **-i-** from **ciento** and that the thousandths take the ending **-ésimo(s).**

Fractions are also expressed by using the feminine form of the ordinal number preceded by a feminine form of either the definite **(la, las)** or indefinite article **(una, unas)** and followed by the noun **parte.**

una quinta parte   *one-fifth*
las dos terceras partes   *two-thirds*
las tres vigésimas partes   *three-twentieths*

FUTURE PERFECT TENSE

The *future perfect tense* is composed of the future tense of **haber** and a past participle. It generally translates *will have . . . , must have . . . ,* or *probably has/have. . . .* Object pronouns come before the forms of **haber.**

Yo **habré vuelto** para mañana.	*I **will have returned** by tomorrow.*
Tú **habrás sabido.**	*You **must have known.***
Él (ella, Ud.) **lo habrá visto.**	*He (she, you) **will have seen it.***
Nosotros **habremos salido.**	*We **will have left.***
Vosotros **habréis entendido.**	*You **will have understood.***
Ellos (Uds.) **le habrán dicho.**	*They (you) **will have told** him.*

In a question, the future perfect tense may translate *I wonder* + present perfect.

¿Adónde **habrán ido**?	*I wonder where **they have gone.***
¿Me **habrán visto**?	*I wonder if **they have seen me.***

FUTURE TENSE

All verbs in Spanish have the following endings in the future tense and most verbs add these endings to the infinitive: **é, ás, á, emos, éis, án.**

yo	hablaré	**nosotros**	hablaremos
tú	hablarás	**vosotros**	hablaréis
él, ella, Ud.	hablará	**ellos, Uds.**	hablarán

The following are the most common irregular verbs in the future tense. They use the same endings as regular verbs but attach them to special stems and not to the infinitive.

Infinitive		**Stem**	
caber	*(to fit)*	**cabr-**	cabré, cabrás, etc.
decir	*(to say, tell)*	**dir-**	diré, dirás, etc.
haber	*(to have)*	**habr-**	habré, habrás, etc.
hacer	*(to make, do)*	**har-**	haré, harás, etc.
poder	*(to be able to)*	**podr-**	podré, podrás, etc.
poner	*(to put)*	**pondr-**	pondré, pondrás, etc.
querer	*(to want)*	**querr-**	querré, querrás, etc.
saber	*(to know)*	**sabr-**	sabré, sabrás, etc.
salir	*(to leave)*	**saldr-**	saldré, saldrás, etc.
tener	*(to have)*	**tendr-**	tendré, tendrás, etc.
valer	*(to be worth)*	**valdr-**	valdré, valdrás, etc.
venir	*(to come)*	**vendr-**	vendré, vendrás, etc.

The common translations of the future tense are *will* and *won't*.

Te diré mañana.	*I **will tell you** tomorrow.*
No iré contigo.	*I **won't go** with you.*

The future tense may translate *probably* + present tense or *must* (in the context of probability). In a question, the future tense may carry the sense of *I wonder.*

Tiene la cara muy roja. **Tomará** mucho.	*He has a red face. He **probably** **drinks** a lot.*
Vivieron dos años en México. **Hablarán** español.	*They lived two years in Mexico. They **must (probably)** speak Spanish.*
¿Cuándo volverán?	*I **wonder when they are returning**.*
¿Me amará?	*I **wonder if she loves me**.*

-GAR *VERBS*

Verbs ending in **-gar** change **-g-** to **-gu-** in the **yo** form of the preterit tense, in all forms of the present subjunctive, and in **usted** and **ustedes** commands, as well as in negative **tú** commands.

PAGAR *(TO PAY)*

Irregular Forms
Preterit: (yo) **pagué**
Present Subjunctive: **pague, pagues, pague, paguemos, paguéis, paguen**
Commands: **pague** Ud., **paguen** Uds., no **pagues** tú

Other common **-gar** verbs include **apagar** *(to turn off),* **cargar** *(to load),* **entregar** *(to hand over),* **llegar** *(to arrive),* **navegar** *(to sail),* and **rogar** *(to beg).*

GENDER: *See NOUNS.*

-GER *AND* -GIR *VERBS*

Verbs ending in **-ger** or **-gir** change **-g-** to **-j-** in the **yo** form of the present indicative, in all forms of the present subjunctive, and in **usted** and **ustedes** commands, as well as in the negative **tú** commands.

DIRIGIR *(TO DIRECT)*

Irregular Forms
Present Indicative: **dirija**
Present Subjunctive: **dirija, dirijas, dirija, dirijamos, dirijáis, dirijan**
Commands: **dirija** Ud., **dirijan** Uds., no **dirijas** tú

Other common **-ger** and **-gir** verbs include **corregir** *(to correct)*, **elegir** *(to elect)*, **escoger** *(to choose)*, **proteger** *(to protect)*, and **recoger** *(to pick up)*.

GERUND

For the formation of gerunds, *see PRESENT PARTICIPLE.*
In English, the *gerund* is the *-ing* form of the verb used as a noun. Spanish tends to use the infinitive as a gerund except when the notion of *by* is implied. *See INFINITIVES.*

Ver es **creer.**	*Seeing* is *believing.*
Escuchando atentamente, uno aprende más.	*(By) listening* attentively, one learns more.
Leyendo las instrucciones primero, hay menos problemas.	*(By) reading* the instructions first, there are fewer problems.

GET

Conseguir *(to get):* For conjugation, *see* -GUIR *VERBS and STEM-CHANGING* -IR *VERBS.*
Obtener *(to get):* For conjugation, *see* TENER.
Obtener and **conseguir** mean *to get* in the sense of *to obtain.*

Obtuvo un mejor puesto.	*She got* a better job.
Consiguieron más apoyo.	*They got* more support.

See BECOME (GET) for a more complete discussion of to get.

-GIR VERBS: See -GER AND -GIR VERBS.

GRAN VS. GRANDE

Gran means *great* and comes before a singular noun. In the plural, **gran** becomes **grandes** and precedes the noun. **Grande(s)** means *large* and comes after the noun.

La reina es una **gran mujer.**	*The queen is a great woman.*
Sheryl Swoopes y Rebecca Lobo son **grandes basquetbolistas.**	*Sheryl Swoopes and Rebecca Lobo are great basketball players.*

La reina es una **mujer grande.**	*The queen is a **large woman.***
La reina y su hermana son **mujeres grandes.**	*The queen and her sister are **large women.***

GREETINGS

The following are some common greetings that are relatively comparable to *Hello, Hi, How are you?, How's it going?,* and the like.

Hola.

¿Cómo le va? (Ud., formal)

¿Qué tal?

¿Qué pasa?

Hola, ¿qué tal?

¿Qué hay?

¿Cómo está? (Ud., formal)

¿Cómo estás? (Tú, familiar)

¿Cómo te va? (Tú, familiar)

¿Qué ha habido?

¿Qué hubo(le)? (Mexico)

¿Qué onda? (Mexico)

-GUAR *VERBS*

Verbs ending in **-guar** change the **-u-** to **-ü-** in the **yo** form of the preterit tense, in all forms of the present subjunctive, and in **usted** and **ustedes** commands as well as in negative **tú** commands.

AVERIGUAR *(TO FIND OUT)*

Irregular Forms

Preterit: (yo) **averigüé**

Present Subjunctive: **averigüe, averigües, averigüe, averigüemos, averigüéis, averigüen**

Commands: **averigüe** Ud., **averigüen** Uds., **no averigües** tú

Apaciguar *(to appease, pacify)* is another **-guar** verb.

-GUIR *VERBS*

Verbs ending in **-guir** drop the **-u-** in the **yo** form of the present indicative, in all forms of the present subjunctive, and in **usted** and **ustedes** commands as well as in negative **tú** commands.

DISTINGUIR *(TO DISTINGUISH)*

Irregular Forms

Present Indicative: **distingo**

Present Subjunctive: **distinga, distingas, distinga, distingamos, distingáis, distingan**

Commands: **distinga** Ud., **distingan** Uds., no **distingas** tú

Other **-guir** verbs include **conseguir** *(to get)*, **extinguir** *(to extinguish)*, **perseguir** *(to pursue)*, and **seguir** *(to follow)*.
See -UIR *VERBS.*

GUSTAR

Spanish uses **gustar** to mean *to like*, but it actually means *to please*. As a result, the subject of the English sentence becomes the object in the Spanish sentence and vice versa.

A la chica le **gustan** las fotos.	*The girl likes the photos.* *(The photos **please** the girl.)*

An indirect object pronoun **(me, te, le, nos, os, les)** is always used with **gustar.** In the previous example, **le** *(to her)* agrees with **la chica,** and **gustan** agrees with **las fotos.** When naming the person being pleased, that is, when using a noun with **gustar, a** always precedes the noun. A singular form of **gustar** is always used when **gustar** is combined with another verb, and the other verb is always an infinitive. For emphasis or clarification, **a** + a prepositional pronoun, usually at the beginning or end of the sentence, may be used with **gustar.**

A los niños les **gusta** el helado.	*The children like the ice cream. (The ice cream **pleases** the children.)*
A mis primos les **gusta** nadar.	*My cousins like to swim. (To swim **pleases** my cousins.)*
A Carlitos le **gusta** comer dulces.	*Carlitos likes to eat candies. (To eat candies **pleases** Carlitos.)*
(A nosotros) nos **gusta** volar.	*We like to fly.*
Les **gustó** la fiesta (a ellos).	*They liked the party.*

(A ella) le **gustan** las sandalias.	*She likes the sandals.*

(A mí) me **gustan** los gatos. ¿Te **gustan** (a ti)?	*I like cats. Do you like them?*

Other verbs used like **gustar** include **doler** *(to hurt, pain, ache)*, **encantar** *(to like very much)*, **faltar** *(to be missing, lack)*, **hacer falta** *(to need)*, **importar** *(to matter)*, **interesar** *(to be interested in)*, **pasar** *(to happen, be the matter)*, **parecer** *(to seem, appear)*, **quedar** *(to have left, remain)*, **sobrar** *(to have left over)*, and **sorprender** *(to be surprised)*.

A mi abuelo le **duelen** las piernas.	*My grandfather's legs **hurt**.*
Le **hacen falta** cincuenta dólares.	*She **needs** fifty dollars.*
Nos **queda** tiempo.	*We **have** time **left**.*

H

HABER *(TO HAVE [AUXILIARY])*

Irregular Forms

Present Indicative: **he, has, ha, hemos, habéis, han**
Preterit: **hube, hubiste, hubo, hubimos, hubisteis, hubieron**
Future: **habré, habrás, habrá, habremos, habréis, habrán**
Conditional: **habría, habrías, habría, habríamos, habríais, habrían**
Present Subjunctive: **haya, hayas, haya, hayamos, hayáis, hayan**
Imperfect Subjunctive: **hubiera,** etc.; **hubiese,** etc.

For HABER (impersonal), *see THERE + TO BE. Also see HAVE:* TENER *VS.* HABER *and PERFECT TENSES.*

HABER DE

Haber de + infinitive is equivalent to the English *to be to* or *to be supposed to.*

Han de regresar mañana.	*They are supposed to return* tomorrow.
He de verlo pronto.	*I am to see him* soon.
Habíamos de terminar ayer.	*We were supposed to finish* yesterday.

Haber de + infinitive may also convey the meaning of *must* in the sense of probability.

Ha de ser rico.	*He must be* rich.

HABER QUE

Haber que + infinitive produces the impersonal forms **hay que** *(it is neces-sary to* or *one must)* and **había que** *(it was necessary to)* as well as similar but less common forms in the other tenses of **haber.**

Hay que pagar al contado.	*It is necessary to pay cash.*
Hay que decir la verdad.	*One must tell the truth.*
Había que escuchar todo.	*It was necessary to listen to everything.*

HABÍA: *See THERE + TO BE.*

HABÍA QUE: *See* HABER QUE.

HACER *(TO MAKE, DO)*

Irregular Forms
Present Indicative: (yo) **hago**
Preterit: **hice, hiciste, hizo, hicimos, hicisteis, hicieron**
Future: **haré, harás, hará, haremos, haréis, harán**
Conditional: **haría, harías, haría, haríamos, haríais, harían**
Present Subjunctive: **haga, hagas, haga, hagamos, hagáis, hagan**
Imperfect Subjunctive: **hiciera,** etc.; **hiciese,** etc.
Imperative: **haz** (tú)
Past Participle: **hecho**

Idiomatic Expressions with *hacer*

hacer caso	*to pay attention*
hacer cola	*to form a line*
hacer daño	*to hurt, harm*
hacer falta	*to be needed, lacking*
hacer frente a	*to face, confront*

hacer juego	*to match, go together*
hacer pedazos	*to break or tear to pieces*
hacer saber	*to inform*
hacer un viaje	*to take a trip*
hacer una maleta	*to pack a suitcase*
hacer una pregunta	*to ask a question*
hacerse atrás	*to move back*
hacerse a un lado	*to move aside*
hacerse el sueco	*to act dumb*
hacerse la vida	*to earn a living*
hacérsele a uno	*to seem, strike*

See WEATHER EXPRESSIONS.

HACER *(IN TIME CLAUSES)*

¿Cuánto tiempo hace que + present tense is equivalent to the English *How long has something been going on* or *How long has somebody been doing some activity.*

¿Cuánto tiempo hace que estudias español?	*How long have you studied (been studying) Spanish?*

Hace + period of time + **que** + a verb in the present tense expresses the English *has/have (been) doing something **for*** a period of time. When the **hace** phrase comes at the end of the sentence, **que** is omitted but may be replaced by **desde.**

Hace tres meses que viven aquí.	*They have lived (been living) here for three months.*
Trabajo con ellos **desde** hace dos años.	*I have worked (been working) with them for two years.*

If both verbs are in the imperfect tense, then the translation is *had* or *had been*.

¿Cuánto tiempo hacía que estudiabas español?	*How long had you studied (been studying) Spanish?*
Hacía tres meses que vivían aquí.	*They had lived (been living) here for three months.*
Trabajaba con ellos (desde) hacía dos años.	*I had worked (been working) with them for two years.*

Hace + a verb in the preterit or imperfect tense is translated as an English sentence ending with *ago*.

Salió **hace** quince minutos.	*He left fifteen minutes **ago**.*
Componían el carro **hace** una hora.	*They were fixing the car an hour **ago**.*

HACERSE: *See BECOME.*

HALF: MEDIO VS. MITAD

Medio means *half* as an adjective. It agrees in number and gender with the noun it modifies and usually precedes it. **Medio** may also be used as an adverb, in which case it is invariable and means *somewhat* or *kind of.*

Deme **medio** kilo de café.	*Give me **half** a kilo of coffee.*
Se peleó con su **media** naranja.	*He had a fight with his better **half**.*
Ella está **medio** loca.	*She is **kind of** crazy.*

Mitad means *half* as a noun.

Puse la otra **mitad** del pastel en el refrigerador.	*I put the other **half** of the pie in the refrigerator.*

HASTA

Hasta as a preposition may mean *up to* or *as far as* when referring to place, *until* or *as late as* when referring to time, and *as much* or *as many as* when referring to quantity. **Hasta** as an adverb means *even.*

Llegaron **hasta** Tucson.	*They got **as far as** Tucson.*
Bailamos **hasta** la medianoche.	*We danced **until** midnight.*
Hay **hasta** mil hombres allí.	*There are **as many as** a thousand men there.*
Creo que ella **hasta** lloró.	*I believe she **even** cried.*

HAVE: TENER *VS.* HABER

For conjugations, *see* TENER *and* HABER.

Both **haber** and **tener** mean *to have*. **Tener** means *to have* in the sense of *to own* or *possess,* and **haber** means *to have* as a helping or auxiliary verb in the perfect tenses.

Tenía mucha paciencia.	***She had** a lot of patience.*
Tiene dos baños.	***It has** two bathrooms.*
Han vuelto temprano.	***They have** returned early.*
Habremos terminado el sábado.	***We will have** finished on Saturday.*

See PERFECT TENSES and TENER.

HAVE TO: See TENER.

HAY: See THERE + TO BE.

HAY QUE: See HABER QUE.

HE: See HABER.

HECHO

Past participle of **hacer** *(to do, to make).*

HELPING VERBS: See HABER *and PERFECT TENSES.*

HERE: ACÁ *VS.* AQUÍ

Aquí means *(right) here,* where the speaker is. **Acá** is used for a less precise location in the vicinity of the speaker and is normally used after verbs indicating movement toward the speaker.

Aquí está el libro que buscaba.	*Here is the book I was looking for.*
¡Juanito! ¡Cuidado con ese caballo! ¡Hazte para **acá**!	*Juanito! Watch out for that horse! Move over **here** (**this way**)!*

HIATUS

Hiatus is when two vowels are together but are pronounced in separate syllables. This occurs when two strong vowels **(a, e, o)** are together or when a **ú** or **í** is stressed (has a written accent) next to a strong vowel **(a-te-o, ca-o-ba, tí-o, pú-a)**.

   See *DIPHTHONGS* and *DIVISION OF WORDS INTO SYLLABLES (SYLLABIFICATION)*.

HOMONYMS

In English, *homonyms* are words that are pronounced the same but spelled differently and have different meanings *(no/know, red/read, bore/boar)*. In Spanish, homonyms frequently have the same spelling **(sé/se, sólo/solo, mí/mi)**. *See ACCENT MARK.*

HOW LONG (TIME): *See HACER (IN TIME CLAUSES).*

HUBO: *See THERE + TO BE.*

I

-IAR VERBS

Some verbs ending in **-iar** require a written accent on the **-í-** of the first, second, and third persons singular and the third-person plural forms of the present indicative and the present subjunctive tenses. The **-i-** is not accented in other tenses.

ENVIAR *(TO SEND)*

Irregular Forms
Present Indicative: **envío, envías, envía,** enviamos, enviáis, **envían**
Present Subjunctive: **envíe, envíes, envíe,** enviemos, enviéis, **envíen**
Commands: **envíe** Ud., **envíen** Uds., **envía** tú, no **envíes** tú

Other **-iar** verbs like **enviar** include **aliar** *(to ally)*, **ampliar** *(to enlarge)*, **confiar** *(to confide)*, **criar** *(to raise)*, **desafiar** *(to challenge)*, **enfriar** *(to cool, chill)*, **espiar** *(to spy)*, **esquiar** *(to ski)*, **fiar** *(to sell on credit)*, **guiar** *(to guide)*, **liar** *(to tie, bind)*, **vaciar** *(to empty)*, and **variar** *(to vary)*.

-iar verbs that do not have accented **-í-** include **anunciar** *(to announce)*, **apreciar** *(to appreciate)*, **cambiar** *(to change)*, **estudiar** *(to study)*, **iniciar** *(to begin)*, **limpiar** *(to clean)*, and **pronunciar** *(to pronounce)*.

IF: *See* SI *CLAUSES.*

IMPERATIVE MOOD: *See* COMMANDS.

IMPERFECT TENSE INDICATIVE

Regular verbs are conjugated in the imperfect tense as follows:

	CANTAR *(TO SING)*	**COMER** *(TO EAT)*
yo	cant**aba**	com**ía**
tú	cant**abas**	com**ías**
él, ella, Ud.	cant**aba**	com**ía**
nosotros	cant**ábamos**	com**íamos**
vosotros	cant**abais**	com**íais**
ellos, Uds.	cant**aban**	com**ían**

Regular **-ir** verbs (**abrir, vivir**) are conjugated like **-er** verbs in the imperfect tense. Only three verbs are irregular in the imperfect tense.

	SER *(TO BE)*	**IR** *(TO GO)*	**VER** *(TO SEE)*
yo	era	iba	veía
tú	eras	ibas	veías
él, ella, Ud.	era	iba	veía
nosotros	éramos	íbamos	veíamos
vosotros	erais	ibais	veíais
ellos, Uds.	eran	iban	veían

In general, the imperfect tense is used (1) to describe scenes, situations, or conditions that existed in the past; (2) to indicate repeated or habitual past actions; (3) to refer to actions in progress in the past; (4) to describe mental activities or states in the past; and (5) to tell time or age in the past. The imperfect tense translates *used to, would* (when referring to the past), and *was/were* + *-ing*. It may also translate the English simple past (*worked, ate, ran,* etc.)

Los cuadros **eran** hermosos.	*The paintings **were** beautiful.*
Yo siempre le **ayudaba.**	*I always **helped** him.*
Pensaban mucho en el problema.	***They thought** a lot about the problem.*
Eran las seis.	*It **was** six o'clock.*
Paco siempre **abrazaba** a su abuelo.	*Paco **would** always **hug** his grandfather.*
Ellos **entraban** y yo **salía.**	*They **were coming in** and I **was going out.***

See PRETERIT VS. IMPERFECT.

IMPERFECT TENSE SUBJUNCTIVE

The imperfect subjunctive for *all* Spanish verbs is formed by removing the **-ron** of the third-person plural of the preterit (abrie**ron**, anduvie**ron**, dije**ron**, habla**ron**, traje**ron**) and adding either the **-ra** or the **-se** endings, the latter being much less common than the former.

DECIR *(TO SAY, TELL)*

dije**ron** *(they said)*

	-ra	*-se*
yo	dije**ra**	dije**se**
tú	dije**ras**	dije**ses**
él, ella, Ud.	dije**ra**	dije**se**
nosotros	dij**éramos**	dij**ésemos**
vosotros	dije**rais**	dije**seis**
ellos, Uds.	dije**ran**	dije**sen**

The formation of the imperfect subjunctive of all Spanish verbs follows the model of **decir.**

The imperfect subjunctive is often translated as an infinitive or as the simple form of the verb in English.

Yo quería que ella **cantara (cantase).**	*I wanted her to sing.*
Insistían en que ella **cantara.**	*They insisted that she sing.*

The imperfect subjunctive also has the following possible translations:

Yo dudaba que ella **cantara (cantase)** aquí.	*I doubted that she (sang, was singing, used to sing, might sing, would sing, did sing) here.*

If a subjunctive tense is required, the imperfect subjunctive is normally used when the expression in the main clause is in a past or conditional tense. The imperfect subjunctive is triggered by the same circumstances and conditions as the present subjunctive:

1. In noun clauses after verbs of volition, permission, request, or the like

Quería que me **dieran** los informes.	*I wanted them to give me the information.*

Insistían en que nos **hospedáramos** en el Hotel Hilton.	*They insisted we stay* at the *Hilton Hotel.*
Me pidió que **volviera** pronto.	*He asked me to return* soon.

2. In noun clauses after verbs of emotion

Yo **sentía** que ella **estuviera** enferma.	*I was sorry she was sick.*
Ella **se alegraba** de que **pudiéramos** ir.	*She was happy we could* go.

3. In noun clauses after verbs expressing disbelief, uncertainty, or doubt

No creían que **fuera** ella.	*They didn't believe it was she.*
Dudaban que les **pagara** pronto.	*They doubted he would pay* them *soon.*

4. In noun clauses after impersonal expressions that convey volition, emotion, doubt, and so on

Era necesario que tú **entendieras** todo.	*It was necessary for you to understand everything.*

5. After **ojalá** *(I wish)*

Ojalá que **viviera** cerca de mí.	*I wish she lived near me.*

6. After **tal vez** and **quizá** or **quizás** to emphasize uncertainty

Tal vez lo **pudieran** hacer.	*Perhaps they could do it.*
Quizá(s) salieran el lunes.	*Maybe they would leave* on Monday.

7. In adjective clauses after indefinite or nonexistent antecedents

No había nadie que **supiera** la respuesta.	*There wasn't anyone who knew the answer.*
Buscaba una pareja que **bailara** bien.	*He was looking for a partner who danced well.*

8. In adverbial clauses after **a fin (de) que** *(so that, in order that)*, **a menos que** *(unless)*, **antes (de) que** *(before)*, **con tal (de) que** *(provided that)*, **en caso (de) que** *(in case)*, **para que** *(so that, in order that)*, and **sin que** *(without)*

Siempre jugaba al golf **a menos que lloviera.**	*He always played golf **unless it rained.***

9. In adverbial clauses after **aunque** *(although, even though)*, **como** *(like, as)*, **cuando** *(when)*, **después de que** *(after)*, **donde** *(where)*, **en cuanto** *(as soon as)*, **hasta que** *(until)*, **luego que** *(as soon as)*, **mientras** *(while)*, and **tan pronto como** *(as soon as)* when the information or action described is not a known or accomplished fact

Yo iría **aunque estuviera** lloviendo.	*I would go **even if it were raining.***
Dijo que me lo iba a decir **en cuanto** lo **supiera.**	*He told me he would let me know **as soon as he found out.***

10. After **como si** *(as if)*

Habla **como si tuviera** mucho dinero.	*He talks **as if he had** a lot of money.*

11. After **si** *(if)* in statements that are contrary to fact

Si viviera con él, no les diría a sus padres.	*If she **lived** with him, she wouldn't tell her parents.*

Note the difference in meaning when the imperfect indicative is used.

Si **vivía** con él, era porque él pagaba todo.	*If she **lived** with him, it was because he paid for everything.*

IMPERFECT TENSE VS. PRETERIT TENSE: *See PRETERIT VS. IMPERFECT.*

IMPERSONAL EXPRESSIONS

Impersonal expressions (it is possible, it was necessary, etc.) do not have a specific person or persons as a subject. Spanish uses a form of **ser** in these formations.

Es posible hacerlo mañana.	*It is possible to do it tomorrow.*
Era necesario llegar a tiempo.	*It was necessary to arrive on time.*

See IMPERFECT TENSE SUBJUNCTIVE and PRESENT TENSE SUBJUNCTIVE.

INDEFINITE ARTICLE

The indefinite articles are (1) masculine singular **un** *(a, an)*, (2) feminine singular **una** *(a, an)*, (3) masculine plural **unos** *(some)*, and (4) feminine plural **unas** *(some)*. The indefinite articles must agree in number and gender with the nouns they modify.

See NOUNS for a discussion of number and gender.

un instituto	*an institute*
una llanta	*a tire*
unos duraznos	*some peaches*
unas brujas	*some witches*

Omission of the Indefinite Article

1. After forms of **ser** with predicate nouns, especially those of nationality, political affiliation, profession, and religion, and frequently after other verbs with direct objects when number is not important.

Es español.	*He's a Spaniard.*
No soy comunista.	*I'm not a communist.*
¿Eres carpintero?	*Are you a carpenter?*
Ella es católica.	*She's a Catholic.*
¿Qué haces? Busco hotel.	*What are you doing? I'm looking for a hotel.*
Necesitas coche para llegar allí.	*You need a car to get there.*

If the predicate noun is modified, the indefinite article is usually used.

Es **un buen** maestro.	*He's **a good** teacher.*

2. After **con** *(with)* and **sin** *(without)*

Lo escribió con pluma.	*He wrote it with **a** pen.*
Llegó sin maleta.	*He arrived without **a** suitcase.*

3. After **tal** *(such a)*

Tal historia es increíble.	*Such **a** story is unbelievable.*

4. After **¡Qué . . . !** meaning *What a . . .*

¡Qué diamante!	*What **a** diamond!*

5. After forms of **no tener**

No tengo bicicleta.	*I don't have **a** bicycle.*

6. After **de** and **como** meaning *as* or *as a/an*

El viejo sirvió de intérprete.	*The old man served as **an** interpreter.*

7. Before the following adjectives: **cien** *(a hundred)*, **ciento** *(a hundred)*, **cierto** *(a certain)*, **medio** *(a half)*, **mil** *(a thousand)*, and **otro** *(another, other)*.

Quiero **otra** falda.	*I want **another** skirt.*
Me dijo **mil** cosas.	*He told me **a thousand** things.*
Me pidió **cierta** receta.	*He asked me for **a certain** recipe.*
Solo quería **media** taza.	*I only wanted **a half** cup.*
Pagué **cien** dólares.	*I paid **a hundred** dollars.*
Costó **ciento** veinte pesetas.	*It cost **a hundred** twenty pesetas.*

INDEFINITES: *See AFFIRMATIVE AND NEGATIVE INDEFINITES.*

INDEPENDENT CLAUSE

An *independent* or *main clause* expresses a complete thought and can stand by itself as a sentence.

Se lo digo cuando ella venga.	*I will tell her when she comes.*

INDICATIVE MOOD VS. SUBJUNCTIVE MOOD

Mood refers to the verb form that is used to indicate how an activity or situation is perceived. In general, the *indicative mood* includes those tenses that ask questions or make statements based on knowledge or perceived facts. A statement in the indicative mood has an independent existence, whereas a statement in the *subjunctive mood* (present and imperfect subjunctive and their compounds) is usually dependent on another expression or thought. The subjunctive mood is generally triggered by desire, emotion, uncertainty, supposition, or a condition that is contrary to fact.

Indicative: Él **está** en casa.   *He is at home.*
Subjunctive: **Ojalá** que él **esté** en casa.   *I hope that he is at home.*

See IMPERFECT TENSE SUBJUNCTIVE, PRESENT PERFECT TENSE SUBJUNCTIVE, PRESENT TENSE SUBJUNCTIVE, and PAST PERFECT SUBJUNCTIVE.

INDIRECT COMMANDS

An indirect command in English is generally introduced by *have* and occasionally by *let, make,* or *may.* In Spanish, **que** followed by the present subjunctive constitutes the indirect command.

Que me lo **traigan** (ellos).	*Have them bring it to me.*
Que (ella) te **diga** la verdad.	*Let her tell you the truth.*
Que Dios te **bendiga.**	*May God bless you.*

Note that direct object, indirect object, and reflexive pronouns always precede indirect commands.

INDIRECT OBJECT PRONOUNS

me	*me*	nos	*us*
te	*you (familiar singular)*	os	*you (familiar plural)*
le	*him, her, you (formal singular)*	les	*them, you (formal plural)*

Indirect object pronouns precede conjugated verbs but are attached to (1) infinitives, (2) present participles, and (3) affirmative commands. Frequently the indirect object pronoun also expresses *to* and *for.*

Yo **te** dije.	*I told **you.***
¿**Me** hablabas?	*Were you talking **to me**?*
No quería manda**rnos** el dinero.	*He didn't want to send **us** the money.*
Estoy leyéndo**le** una carta.	*I'm reading **her** a letter.*
Da**les** una explicación.	*Give **them** an explanation.*
Te compuse la computadora.	*I fixed the computer **for you.***

Sometimes a clarifying or emphatic prepositional phrase with **a** + a prepositional pronoun is used with an indirect object pronoun. These prepositional phrases are used in addition to the indirect object pronoun; they do not replace it.

Le dijeron **a él.**	*They told **him.***
No **me** hablaron **a mí.**	*They didn't speak **to me**.*

The Redundant Indirect Object Pronoun

Even though the indirect object is a noun, a seemingly redundant indirect object pronoun is normally used in Spanish.

Les di el regalo **a los niños.**	*I gave the present **to the kids.***
Voy a mostrar**le** la factura **a José.**	*I am going to show the invoice **to José.***

When a direct object pronoun and an indirect object pronoun are used together, the indirect object pronoun comes before the direct object regardless of their order in the English sentence. If the indirect object pronoun is **le** or **les,** it is changed to **se**. Frequently a prepositional phrase (**a él, a ella, a ellas, a ellos, a Ud., a Uds.**) is used to clarify **se**.

Nos lo compró.	*He bought **it for us**.*
Me los va a mostrar.	*He is going to show **them to me**.*
Te los abrí.	*I opened **them for you**.*
Se la mandé.	*I sent it **to (you, him, her, them)**.*

See DIRECT OBJECT PRONOUNS.

Special Use of the Indirect Object Pronoun

When forms of **ser** are used impersonally, an indirect object pronoun is sometimes used to identify the person(s) to whom the impersonal expression refers.

Nos es difícil llegar a tiempo.	*It is **difficult for us** to arrive on time.*
Le fue imposible terminar el trabajo.	*It **was impossible for him** to finish the work.*

However, it is more common to use a subordinate clause with impersonal expressions.

Es difícil que lleguemos a tiempo.	*It is difficult for us to arrive on time.*
Fue imposible que terminara el trabajo.	*It was impossible for him to finish the work.*

See PRESENT TENSE SUBJUNCTIVE.

INFINITIVE

In English, the infinitive is *to* + the simple form of the verb: *to play, to sing, to stir,* and so on. In Spanish, all infinitives end in **-ar** (**pesar** *to weigh*), **-er** (**lamer** *to lick*) or **-ir** (**escupir** *to spit*). In general, infinitives are used with a conjugated verb. Object pronouns can be attached to infinitives.

No podían **creer** eso.	*They weren't able **to believe** that.*
No quiero **quejarme**.	*I don't want **to complain**.*
Pensaba **decirte** mañana.	*I intended **to tell you** tomorrow.*

Special Uses of the Infinitive

After prepositions, the infinitive and not the present participle is used.

Se acostó **después de leer** el periódico.	*She went to bed **after reading** the newspaper.*
Antes de volver a casa, voy a tomar un refresco.	***Before returning** home I'm going to have a soft drink.*
Estoy cansado **de escucharte.**	*I'm tired **of listening to you.***
¿Por qué te fuiste **sin decirme**?	*Why did you go **without telling me**?*

After Verbs of the Senses

Me **vio salir.**	*He saw me **leave (leaving).***
Te **oí llegar.**	*I heard you **arrive (arriving).***

As Impersonal Negative Commands

NO **FUMAR**	*NO SMOKING*
NO **PISAR** EL CÉSPED	*DON'T WALK ON GRASS.*
NO **ESTACIONARSE**	*NO PARKING*

As a Substitute for a Gerund

(El) **Vivir** en un desierto es difícil.	***Living** in a desert is hard.*
Ayudar a los ancianos no cuesta nada.	***Helping** the elderly doesn't cost anything.*

INTERROGATIVES

¿Adónde?	*Where?*
¿Cómo?	*How?*
¿Cuál, Cuáles?	*What, which, which one, which ones?*
¿Cuándo?	*When?*

¿Cuánto(-a)?	*How much?*
¿Cuántos(-as)?	*How many?*
¿De dónde?	*Where?*
¿Dónde?	*Where?*
¿Qué?	*What?*
¿Quién(es)?	*Who? Whom?*

The interrogatives have a written accent mark in direct or indirect questions and in exclamations. When they are not used as question or exclamatory words, they do not have accent marks.

¿**Cuándo** llegaste?	***When** did you arrive?*
¿**Qué** quería?	***What** did he want?*
¿**Cómo** lo supiste?	***How** did you find out?*
¡**Qué** lata!	***What** a problem!*
No sabe **dónde** lo puso.	*He doesn't know **where** he put it.*
Me dijo **donde** tú vives.	*He told me **where** you live.*
Me mostró el regalo **que** te compró.	*He showed me the present **that** he bought you.*

Where? ¿adónde / de dónde / dónde?

¿**Dónde?** is the most common expression for *where.*

¿**Dónde** viven?	***Where** do they live?*
¿**Dónde** lo hallaste?	***Where** did you find it?*

¿**Adónde?** is used with verbs that indicate movement from one place to another, primarily **ir** and **llevar.**

¿**Adónde** vas?	***Where** are you going?*
¿**Adónde** lo llevaron?	***Where** did they take him?*

¿**De dónde?** is primarily used to ask where someone or something is from.

¿**De dónde** eres?	***Where*** *are you from?*
¿**De dónde** eran?	***Where*** *were they from?*

Who(m)? ¿quién/quiénes?

Who or *whom* in Spanish may be either the singular ¿**quién?** or the plural ¿**quiénes?** When used as objects of verbs, both are preceded by **a.**

¿**Quién** viene?	***Who's*** *coming?*
¿**Quiénes** vienen?	***Who's*** *coming?*
¿**A quién** viste?	***Who(m)*** *did you see?*

See WHOSE: CUYO *VS.* ¿DE QUIÉN(ES)?

Why? / Because ¿por qué? / porque

¿**Por qué?** is *why,* and **porque** is *because.*

¿**Por qué** te fuiste temprano?	***Why*** *did you leave early?*
Porque estaba cansado.	***Because*** *I was tired.*

How Much? / How Many? ¿cuánto(a)? / ¿cuántos(as)?

Like other adjectives, **cuánto(a)** must agree with the noun it modifies.

¿**Cuánto** dinero hay?	***How much*** *money is there?*
¿**Cuánta** paciencia tiene?	***How much*** *patience does she have?*
¿**Cuántos** boletos necesitas?	***How many*** *tickets do you need?*
¿**Cuántas** libras quieres?	***How many*** *pounds do you want?*

What?/Which? ¿qué?/¿cuál?

For a definition or explanation, ¿**qué?** is used. For a choice, ¿**cuál?** or ¿**cuáles?** is used. However, ¿**qué?** is used before a noun.

¿**Qué** es un berro?	*What's watercress?*
¿**Qué** necesitas?	*What do you need?*
¿**Cuál** es la capital?	*What is the capital?*
¿**Cuál** necesitas?	*Which one do you need?*
¿**Cuáles** buscabas?	*Which ones were you looking for?*
¿**Qué** globo quieres?	*Which balloon do you want?*

See RELATIVE PRONOUNS and CUÁL VS. QUÉ.

INTRODUCE: PRESENTAR *VS.* INTRODUCIR

For conjugation of **introducir**, *see* -DUCIR *VERBS.*

Presentar means *to introduce* one person to another, and **introducir** means *to introduce* in the sense of inserting something or showing something.

Me **presentó** a su abuela.	*He **introduced** me to his grandmother.*
Ford va a **introducir** su nuevo modelo en abril.	*Ford is going to **introduce** its new model in April.*
El cirujano le **introdujo** el aparato.	*The surgeon **introduced (inserted)** the device.*

IR *(TO GO)*

Irregular Forms

Present Indicative: **voy, vas, va, vamos, vais, van**
Preterit: **fui, fuiste, fue, fuimos, fuisteis, fueron**
Imperative Indicative: **iba, ibas, iba, íbamos, ibais, iban**
Present Subjunctive: **vaya, vayas, vaya, vayamos, vayáis, vayan**
Imperfect Subjunctive: **fuera, fueras,** etc.; **fuese, fueses,** etc.
Imperative: **ve**
Present Participle: **yendo**

When a form of **ir** is followed by an infinitive, **a** is required before the infinitive.

¿Qué vas **a** hacer?	*What are you going to do?*
Fue **a** trabajar.	*She went to work.*
Iba **a** decirte.	*I was going to tell you.*

Spanish often uses forms of **ir** in place of **estar** in the formation of the progressive tenses, especially when the activity described is gradually being accomplished.

Él **va mejorando** su español poco a poco.	*He is improving his Spanish little by little.*

Idiomatic Expressions with *ir*

ir a caballo	*to ride a horse*
ir a pie	*to walk*
ir de brazo	*to walk arm in arm*
ir de caza	*to go hunting*
ir de compras	*to go shopping*
ir de paseo	*to go for a stroll or ride*
ir de pesca	*to go fishing*
irse abajo	*to collapse*

IRREGULAR VERBS

Irregular verbs are those that do not follow the normal conjugation pattern in one or more tenses. For example, **ir** *(to go)* and **caber** *(to fit)* are irregular verbs in the present tense indicative:
ir: voy, vas, va, vamos, vais, van
caber: quepo, cabes, cabe, cabemos, cabéis, caben

See PRESENT TENSE INDICATIVE.

-ÍSIMO: *See VERY.*

IT: *See DIRECT OBJECT PRONOUNS,* ELLO, LO, *and SUBJECT PRONOUNS.*

J

JUGAR *(TO PLAY)*

Irregular Forms
Present Indicative: **juego, juegas, juega,** jugamos, jugáis, **juegan**
Preterit: **jugué,** jugaste, jugó, jugamos, jugasteis, jugaron
Present Subjunctive: **juegue, juegues, juegue, juguemos, juguéis, jueguen**

When **jugar** has an object, it is generally followed by **a** or **al.**

Jugaba a la ruleta.	*I was playing roulette.*
¿Te gusta **jugar a** las damas?	*Do you like **to play** checkers?*
Jugaron al tenis anoche.	*They played tennis last night.*
De niño, **jugaba al** béisbol.	*As a child, **I used to play** baseball.*

See PLAY: JUGAR *VS.* TOCAR.

JUST

Just, in the sense of *fair* or *equitable,* is **justo,** and in the sense of *only, just* may be **sólo, solamente,** or **únicamente.** *Just (about),* meaning *almost,* is **casi,** and *just* meaning *exactly* can be **exactamente, precisamente,** or **justamente.**

El fallo del juez fue **justo.**	*The decision of the judge was **just** (fair).*
—Soy **sólo** un empleado, señora.	*"I'm **just** (only) a clerk, ma'am."*
Me quitaron **casi** todo.	*They took away **just about** everything.*
Eso es **precisamente** lo que le dije.	*That is **just** (exactly) what I told him.*

For *have (has) just, see* ACABAR DE.

K

KNOW: SABER *VS.* CONOCER

For conjugations, *see* SABER *and* -CER *AND* -CIR *VERBS*.
Conocer means *to know* in the sense of *to be familiar* or *acquainted with*.
Saber means *to know* in the sense of *to know a fact, to know something,* or *to know how to do something.*

No **conozco** a tus padres.	*I don't **know** your parents.*
¿**Conoces** esta revista?	*Do you **know** this magazine?*
Conocen Nueva York.	*They **know** New York.*
Tere **sabe** la dirección.	*Tere **knows** the address.*
No **saben** dónde vivo.	*They don't **know** where I live.*
¿**Sabes** jugar al dominó?	*Do you **know** how to play dominoes?*
No **sé** patinar.	*I don't **know** how to skate.*

L

LA(S): *See DIRECT OBJECT PRONOUNS and DEFINITE ARTICLES.*

LAST

Last in a time framework is expressed by the definite article (**el, la**) + time period + **pasado(a).** *Last night,* however, is **anoche.** In a series, *last* is **último(a).**

el año **pasado**	*last year*
la primavera **pasada**	*last spring*
el último rey	*the last king*

LATTER: *See DEMONSTRATIVE ADJECTIVES AND PRONOUNS.*

LE(S): *See INDIRECT OBJECT PRONOUNS.*

LEAVE: DEJAR VS. SALIR

For conjugation, *see SALIR.*
To leave meaning *to exit* or *to go out* is **salir (de),** and *to leave someone* or *something* is **dejar.**

Salió de la oficina hace una hora.	*She left the office an hour ago.*
Ya no **sale** con él.	*She doesn't go out with him anymore.*
Dejé el paquete en el baúl.	*I left the package in the trunk.*
Déjeme en paz.	*Leave me alone.*

LEER *(TO READ)*

For conjugation, *see* -EER *VERBS.*

LEÍSMO

Leísmo is the use of **le** as a singular masculine direct object instead of **lo.**

Le veo.	*I see **him.***
Lo veo.	*I see **him.***

See DIRECT OBJECT PRONOUNS and *INDIRECT OBJECT PRONOUNS.*

LET

Let, meaning *to grant* or *request permission,* is expressed by a form of either **dejar** or **permitir** and should not be confused with the *let's* construction.

Mi padre me **deja (permite)** manejar su coche.	*My father **lets** me drive his car.*

See DEJAR (DE), *INDIRECT COMMANDS,* and *LET'S.*

LET'S

Let's may be expressed by **vamos a** + infinitive:

Vamos a salir.	*Let's leave.*
Vamos a levantarnos.	*Let's get up.*
Vamos a hablarle.	*Let's talk to him.*
Vamos a hacerlo.	*Let's do it.*

Let's may also be expressed by the **nosotros** form of the present subjunctive. *See PRESENT TENSE SUBJUNCTIVE.* Pronoun objects follow and are attached. Reflexive verbs (*see REFLEXIVE VERBS*) drop the **-s** of the **nosotros** forms of the present subjunctive and add **-nos.**

Salgamos.	*Let's leave.*
Hablémosle.	*Let's talk to him.*
Comámoslos.	*Let's eat them.*
Hagámoslo.	*Let's do it.*
Sentémonos.	*Let's sit down.*
Vistámonos.	*Let's get dressed.*
Levantémonos.	*Let's get up.*

Let's not is expressed by **no** + the **nosotros** form of the present subjunctive. Pronoun objects precede the verb.

No salgamos.	*Let's not leave.*
No le hablemos.	*Let's not talk to him.*
No los comamos.	*Let's not eat them.*
No lo hagamos.	*Let's not do it.*
No nos sentemos.	*Let's not sit down.*
No nos vistamos.	*Let's not get dressed.*
No nos levantemos.	*Let's not get up.*

Let's go and *let's go away* are exceptions in that the **nosotros** form of the present indicative is used instead of the present subjunctive. However, the present subjunctive is used for *let's not go* and *let's not go away.*

Vamos.	*Let's go.*
Vámonos.	*Let's (leave) go away.*
No vayamos.	*Let's not go.*
No nos vayamos.	*Let's not (leave) go away.*

Let's see can be translated three ways.

Vamos a ver.	*Let's see.*
Veamos.	*Let's see.*
A ver.	*Let's see.*

LIKE: See GUSTAR.

LINKING

Linking is the tendency in English and Spanish to speak (pronounce) in syllables and not in words. For example, if the final sound of a syllable or a word is a consonant followed by a syllable that begins with a vowel sound, the final consonant is pronounced in the syllable with the following vowel. As a result, the English *keep it* is pronounced *kee pit,* and the Spanish **es azul** is pronounced **e sazul.**

LITTLE

Little meaning *small in size* is usually expressed by a form of either **pequeño** or **chico.** *Little in quantity* is **(un) poco,** which in its plural form means *(a) few.* **Poco** may also be used as an adverb.

Compró una bolsa **pequeña.**	*She bought a **small** purse.*
Las horquillas **chicas** están en el estuche.	*The **small** hairpins are in the case.*
Tengo **poco** dinero.	*I have **little** money.*
¿Quieres pastel? Sí, dame **un poco.**	*Do you want cake? Yes, give me a **little**.*
Hay **pocas** oportunidades.	*There are **few** chances.*
Comiste **poco.**	*You ate **little**.*

LLANA (PALABRA)

A **palabra llana** is a word whose stress is on the next-to-last (penult) syllable (difícil, **ha**bla, ca**mi**sa, etc.). *See ACCENT MARK.*

LLEGAR *(TO ARRIVE)*

For conjugation, *see* -GAR *VERBS*.
Llegar meaning *to arrive in* or *at* is followed by **a** and not **en.**

Llegó a Chicago anoche.	*She arrived in Chicago last night.*
Vamos a **llegar a** la playa mañana.	*We are going **to arrive at** the beach tomorrow.*

LO

Lo may be used in Spanish as a pronoun or as a neuter article.

Pronoun

1. As a masculine direct object meaning *him, you,* or *it*

¿Tienes el saldo? Sí, **lo** tengo.	*Do you have the balance? Yes I have **it.***
¿**Lo** conozco?	*Do I know **you**?*
¿**Lo** viste?	*Did you see **him**?*

See DIRECT OBJECT PRONOUNS.

2. As a neuter direct object meaning *it*

Está muerto. No **lo** creo.	*He's dead. I don't believe **it**.*
Me quiere mucho. **Lo** sé.	*She loves me a lot. I know **it**.*

3. With **ser** and **estar** to refer to a preceding noun or adjective

¿Es tu **profesor?** Sí, **lo** es.	*Is he your teacher? Yes, he is.*
¿Estás **cansada?** Sí, **lo** estoy.	*Are you tired? Yes, I am.*

The impersonal forms of the verb **haber** are also commonly used with an object pronoun. However, the pronoun agrees in number and gender with the predicate.

¿Hay muchas **personas** allí? Sí, **las** hay.	*Are there many people there? Yes, there are.*

4. With **saber** + **todo**

Lo sabe todo.	*He knows everything (it all).*

5. In the formation of the relative pronouns **lo que** or **lo cual,** meaning *what* or *(that) which*

Lo que me dijo no era cierto.	***What** he told me wasn't true.*
Gastó todo su dinero en el hipódromo, **lo cual** no le gustó a su mujer.	*He spent all his money at the racetrack, **which** didn't please his wife.*

See RELATIVE PRONOUNS.

6. With **de** + a noun, an infinitive, or an adverb to mean *that matter of* or *that business about*

No te preocupes por **lo de** anoche.	*Don't worry about (**that matter of**) last night.*

Neuter Article

1. As a neuter article with the masculine singular form of the adjective or possessive pronoun meaning *what is . . .* or *the . . . thing*

Lo cierto es que no te quiere.	***What is certain** is that he doesn't love you.*
Lo interesante fue que se acordó de mí.	***The interesting thing** was that she remembered me.*
Lo importante es estudiar todo.	***The important thing** is to study everything.*
Lo mío se queda conmigo.	***What is mine** stays with me.*
Puedes vender **lo tuyo.**	*You can sell **what is yours.***

2. Before adverbs or adjectives to translate *how* when it expresses a degree

Es increíble **lo fuertes** que son.	*It's incredible **how strong** they are.*
Me sorprende **lo temprano** que se levantó.	*I'm surprised at **how early** he got up.*

3. In numerous idiomatic expressions

a lo largo de	*along*
a lo lejos	*in the distance*
a lo mejor	*probably*
por lo general	*generally*
por lo pronto	*for the time being*
por lo tanto	*consequently*
por lo visto	*apparently*

LO QUE (CUAL): *See RELATIVE PRONOUNS.*

LOÍSMO

Loísmo is the use of **lo** as a singular masculine indirect object instead of **le.**

Lo dije.	*I told **him**.*
Le dije.	*I told **him**.*

See DIRECT OBJECT PRONOUNS and *INDIRECT OBJECT PRONOUNS.*

LOS: *See DIRECT OBJECT PRONOUNS and DEFINITE ARTICLES.*

M

MAIN CLAUSE: *See INDEPENDENT CLAUSE.*

MAL(O) (BAD/SICK)

The adjective **malo** becomes **mal** before a masculine singular noun. In other positions, **malo** has normal adjectival endings. *See ADJECTIVES.*
Mal is also the adverbial form. With forms of **estar, malo** usually means *sick*.

Tiene un **mal** genio.	*He has a **bad** temperament.*
Tiene un genio **malo.**	*He has a **bad** temperament.*
Maldijo su **mala** suerte.	*He cursed his **bad** luck.*
Se sintió **mal.**	*He felt **bad.***
¿Estuviste **malo** ayer?	*Were you **sick** yesterday?*

MASCULINE WORDS: *See NOUNS, DEFINITE ARTICLES, and INDEFINITE ARTICLES.*

MAY

May meaning *a request for* or *a granting of permission* is a form of the present indicative of **poder. Es posible que, tal vez, quizá(s),** or **acaso** + the present subjunctive renders *may* suggesting possibility, and in a dependent clause, the present subjunctive also renders *may*. *See PRESENT TENSE SUBJUNCTIVE and INDIRECT COMMANDS.*

¿**Puedo** sentarme?	*May I sit down?*
Ya **puedes** retirarte.	*You **may** leave now.*
Es posible que no me **reconozca.**	*She **may** not **recognize** me.*
Tal vez te **den** los resultados mañana.	*They **may give** you the results tomorrow.*
Acaso estén rotos.	*They **may** be broken.*
Tiene miedo de que no **lleguemos** a tiempo.	*He's afraid we **may** not **arrive** on time.*
Que en paz **descanse.**	***May** he **rest** in peace.*

MAYBE

Puede ser, acaso, quizá(s), and **tal vez** mean *maybe (perhaps),* and when emphasizing uncertainty, each is followed by the subjunctive. **A lo mejor** can also convey *maybe,* but it is usually followed by the indicative.

Tal vez no **sepa** manejar.	***Maybe he doesn't know** how to drive.*
Quizá(s) ya **se hayan** ido.	***Maybe they have** already **gone.***
Puede ser que **tengan** prisa.	***Maybe they are** in a hurry.*
A lo mejor son hermanos.	***Maybe they are** brothers.*

MAYOR(ES): *See COMPARATIVES and SUPERLATIVES.*

ME: *See DIRECT OBJECT PRONOUNS, INDIRECT OBJECT PRONOUNS, and REFLEXIVE PRONOUNS.*

MEASUREMENTS

Spanish-speaking countries use the metric system.

Linear Measures

1 **centímetro** *(centimeter)* = 0.3937 **pulgada** *(inch)*
1 **metro** *(meter)* = 39.37 **pulgadas** *(inches)*
1 **kilómetro** *(kilometer)* = 0.6214 **milla** *(mile)*

Measure of Capacity

1 **litro** *(liter)* = 1.057 **cuartos** *(quarts)*

Surface Measures

1 **centímetro cuadrado** *(square centimeter)* = 0.155 **pulgada cuadrada** *(square inch)*
1 **metro cuadrado** *(square meter)* = 10.764 **pies cuadrados** *(square feet)*
1 **hectárea** *(hectare)* = 2.47 *acres*
1 **kilómetro cuadrado** *(square kilometer)* = 247.1 *acres*

Weight

1 **gramo** *(gram)* = 0.035 **onza** *(ounce)*
1 **kilo** *(kilogram)* = 2.2046 **libras** *(pounds)*

MEDIO: *See HALF:* MEDIO *VS.* MITAD.

MEET: CONOCER VS. ENCONTRARSE (CON)

For conjugations, *see* -CER *AND* -CIR *VERBS and* STEM-CHANGING *VERBS:* -AR *AND* -ER.

Conocer translates as *to meet* in the sense of being introduced to someone, and **encontrarse con** means *to meet* in the sense of casually meeting or running into someone.

Quiere **conocer** a mi hermana.	*He wants **to meet** my sister.*
Me encontré con mi viejo adversario en el hipódromo.	*I **met** (**ran into**) my old adversary at the horse track.*

See CONOCER.

MEJOR(ES): *See* COMPARATIVES *and* SUPERLATIVES.

MENOR(ES): *See* COMPARATIVES *and* SUPERLATIVES.

-MENTE: *See* ADVERBS.

MI(S): *See POSSESSIVE ADJECTIVES.*

MÍ: *See PREPOSITIONAL PRONOUNS and REFLEXIVE PRONOUNS.*

MÍO (MÍA, MÍOS, MÍAS): *See POSSESSIVE ADJECTIVES and POSSESSIVE PRONOUNS.*

MONTHS

enero	*January*	julio	*July*
febrero	*February*	agosto	*August*
marzo	*March*	septiembre, setiembre	*September*
abril	*April*	octubre	*October*
mayo	*May*	noviembre	*November*
junio	*June*	diciembre	*December*

The months are not capitalized in Spanish. *See DATES.*

MOOD (VERBS): *See INDICATIVE (MOOD) VS. SUBJUNCTIVE (MOOD).*

MORE: *See COMPARATIVES.*

MORIR *(TO DIE)*

For conjugation, *see STEM-CHANGING VERBS:* -IR *and* MUERTO.

MOST: *See SUPERLATIVE.*

MOVE: MOVERSE VS. MUDARSE/CAMBIARSE

To physically move around is **moverse,** and *to move* in the sense of changing one's place of residence is either **mudarse** or **cambiarse.**

Para bailar salsa **se mueve** todo el cuerpo.	*To dance salsa, **you move** your whole body.*

Se movió rápido cuando le habló su papá.	*He moved really quickly when his father spoke to him.*
Voy a **mudarme** a otra casa este fin de semana.	*I'm going to move to another house this weekend.*
¿Por qué **te cambiaste** de tu apartamento?	*Why did you move from your apartment?*

For conjugation of **moverse,** see *STEM-CHANGING VERBS: -AR AND -ER. Also see REFLEXIVE VERBS.*

MR. AND MRS.

Los señores Gómez ya no viven aquí.	*Mr. and Mrs. Gómez no longer live here.*
Los señores Losada trabajan con la misma empresa.	*Mr. and Mrs. Losada work with the same company.*

See ABBREVIATIONS and DEFINITE ARTICLES.

MUCHO

Mucho may serve as an adjective or as an adverb. As an adjective, it means *much, a lot of,* or *many.* It precedes the noun it modifies and agrees with it in gender and number. **Mucho** as an adverb means *much* or *a lot* and is invariable.

Ellos tienen **mucho** dinero.	*They have a lot of money.*
Hay **muchas** hojas en la acera.	*There are many leaves on the sidewalk.*
Este libro es **mucho** más interesante que el otro.	*This book is much more interesting than the other one.*
Ella trabaja **mucho.**	*She works a lot.*

MUERTO *(DIED/DEAD)*

Muerto is the past participle of **morir** *(to die).*

No ha **muerto** todavía.	*He hasn't **died** yet.*
¡Cuidado! Están **muertos**.	*Be careful! They're **dead**.*

See PAST PARTICIPLE and PERFECT TENSES.

MUST: *See* TENER *and FUTURE TENSE.*

MUY: *See VERY.*

N

NADA: *See AFFIRMATIVE AND NEGATIVE INDEFINITES.*

NADIE: *See AFFIRMATIVE AND NEGATIVE INDEFINITES.*

NATIONALITIES: *See ADJECTIVES.*

NEGATION

Spanish has no negative auxiliaries like the English *didn't, doesn't, won't,* and so on. *Negation* is achieved in Spanish by simply putting **no** before the main verb or before the helping verb in the perfect tenses. If the verb is preceded by a direct object pronoun, indirect object pronoun, or a reflexive pronoun, **no** comes before the pronoun. A negative response to a yes-or-no question requires two **no**s.

No molió el café.	*He **didn't grind** the coffee.*
Ella **no escucha** a sus padres.	*She **doesn't listen** to her parents.*
Yo **no he visto** esa película.	*I **haven't seen** that movie.*
El preso **no se escapó.**	*The prisoner **didn't escape.***
Ellos **no me lo han contado.**	*They **haven't told me.***
¿Vas al concierto? **No, no voy.**	*Are you going to the concert? **No, I'm not going.***
¿Pagaste la cuenta? **No, no la pagué.**	*Did you pay the bill? **No, I didn't pay it.***

See also AFFIRMATIVE AND NEGATIVE INDEFINITES.

NEUTER ARTICLE/PRONOUN: *See LO.*

NEXT

In a chronological time sequence, **el (la)** + time frame + **que** + **viene (entra)** renders *next*.

el mes **que viene**	*next month*
la semana **que entra**	*next week*
el verano **que viene**	*next summer*

Próximo means *next* in either a time sequence or a series.

el año **próximo**	*next year*
su **próximo** novio	*her next boyfriend*
mi **próxima** casa	*my next house*

When indicating one's readiness to receive someone, such as a doctor for a patient or a business person for a customer, the following is used:

—El (la) que sigue.   *"Next."*

NI: *See AFFIRMATIVE AND NEGATIVE INDEFINITES.*

NINGUN(O): *See AFFIRMATIVE AND NEGATIVE INDEFINITES, ANY, and* CUALQUIER(A).

NOS: *See DIRECT OBJECT PRONOUNS, INDIRECT OBJECT PRONOUNS, and REFLEXIVE PRONOUNS.*

NOSOTROS(AS): *See PREPOSITIONAL PRONOUNS, REFLEXIVE PRONOUNS, and SUBJECT PRONOUNS.*

NOUN CLAUSE

A *noun clause* is a group of words that contains a subject and verb (predicate) but does not express a complete thought. The clause functions as a noun in the sentence, and in Spanish most often serves as a direct object.

| Espero **que él sepa la verdad.** | *I hope (that) he knows the truth.* |

NOUNS

All Spanish *nouns* have gender (feminine or masculine) and number (singular or plural).

Pluralization

Nouns ending in a vowel (except **í**) add **-s** to form the plural.

caja	*box*	cajas	*boxes*
palo	*stick*	palos	*sticks*
parche	*patch*	parches	*patches*

Nouns ending in **í** usually add **-es**.

| colibrí | *hummingbird* | colibríes | *hummingbirds* |
| rubí | *ruby* | rubíes | *rubies* |

Nouns ending in a consonant add **-es** to form the plural.

mantel	*tablecloth*	manteles	*tablecloths*
reloj	*clock*	relojes	*clocks*
ley	*law*	leyes	*laws*

Nouns ending in **-án, -én, -ión,** or **-és** drop the accent mark in the plural.
Nouns ending in **-z** change **-z-** to **-c-** before adding **-es**.

| canción | *song* | canciones | *song* |
| nuez | *nut* | nueces | *nuts* |

Nouns of more than one syllable that end in an unaccented **-es** or **-is** are the same in the singular and plural. However, single-syllable nouns ending in **-es** and polysyllabic nouns ending in accented **-és** are pluralized by adding **-es**.

el lunes	*Monday*	los lunes	*Mondays*
la crisis	*the crisis*	las crisis	*the crises*
el mes	*the month*	los meses	*the months*
el inglés	*the Englishman*	los ingleses	*the English*

Compound nouns with a singular form ending in **-s** have the same form in the plural.

el abrelatas	*the can opener*	**los** abrelatas	*the can openers*
el paraguas	*the umbrella*	**los** paraguas	*the umbrellas*

Gender

The endings of many Spanish nouns may indicate whether the noun is masculine or feminine. The following classifications of endings should prove helpful, but the gender of many nouns in Spanish cannot be determined by their endings and must therefore be learned individually.

Common Masculine Endings

The most common ending for masculine nouns is **-o.**

un refresco	*a soft drink*
el negocio	*the business*
el chaleco	*the vest*
un florero	*a vase*

Common exceptions are **la mano** *(the hand)*, **la radio** *(the radio)*, and abbreviated forms such as **la foto** for **la fotografía** *(the photo)*, **la moto** for **la motocicleta** *(the motorcycle)*, and **la disco** for **la discoteca** *(the discotheque).*

A few nouns ending in **-o** may be masculine or feminine depending on whether they refer to a male or female person.

el/la modelo	*the model*
el/la reo	*the criminal*
el/la soprano	*the soprano*
el/la testigo	*the witness*

It is much more common, however, for nouns ending in **-o** that refer to persons (or animals) to change the **-o** to **-a** to indicate the feminine.

un gat**o**	*a tomcat*	una gat**a**	*a female cat*
mi prim**o**	*my male cousin*	mi prim**a**	*my female cousin*
el abogad**o**	*the male lawyer*	la abogad**a**	*the female lawyer*

Nouns ending in **-or** that refer to people are masculine. The feminine is formed by adding **-a** to the masculine form.

el profesor	*the male professor*	la profesor**a**	*the female professor*
el director	*the male director*	la director**a**	*the female director*

Many nouns ending in **-ma** which have English cognates are masculine.

el drama	*the drama*	el sistema	*the system*
el problema	*the problem*	el telegrama	*the telegram*

Other nouns in this group include **aroma** *(aroma)*, **clima** *(climate)*, **idioma** *(language)*, **programa** *(program)*, and **tema** *(theme)*.

Common Feminine Endings

Most nouns ending in **-a** are feminine.

la per**a**	*the pear*
una estrell**a**	*a star*

Common exceptions, besides the previously mentioned cognates ending in **-ma,** include **el día** *(the day),* **el mapa** *(the map),* **el planeta** *(the planet),* and **el tranvía** *(the streetcar).*

Nouns that end in **-ción, -dad, -sión, -tad, -tud,** and **-umbre** are feminine.

la emo**ción**	*the emotion*	la liber**tad**	*freedom*
una mal**dad**	*an evil act*	la juven**tud**	*youth*
la diver**sión**	*the fun*	una leg**umbre**	*a vegetable*

Most nouns ending in **-d** or **-ie** are feminine.

una pare**d**	*a wall*
la ser**ie**	*the series*

Some exceptions to this rule include **el ataúd** *(the coffin)* and **el pie** *(the foot).*

Nouns ending in **-ista** and **-ta** that refer to people and have English cognates may be masculine or feminine depending on whether they refer to a masculine or feminine person.

el/la art**ista**	*the artist*
el/la comentar**ista**	*the commentator*
el/la astronau**ta**	*the astronaut*

Feminine nouns beginning with a stressed **a-** or **ha-** require the definite article **el** instead of **la.** The indefinite article **una** is used with these nouns, but **un** is also considered permissible. They follow the pattern of feminine words in all other aspects, including agreement of adjectives and plural forms.

el agua sucia	*the dirty water*
las **ha**chas filosas	*the sharp axes*

el alma perdida	*the lost soul*
el hambre	*hunger*
un(a) **a**rpa	*a harp*

Other words that follow this pattern include **águila** *(eagle)*, **ama** *(lady of the house)*, **aula** *(classroom)*, and **ave** *(bird)*.

Some nouns may be either masculine or feminine, with a corresponding change in meaning.

el capital	*capital—money*	la capital	*capital—city*
el cometa	*comet*	la cometa	*kite*
el cólera	*cholera*	la cólera	*anger*
el corte	*cut*	la corte	*court*
el cura	*priest*	la cura	*cure*
el frente	*front—war*	la frente	*forehead*
el guía	*guide—person*	la guía	*handbook, female guide*
el orden	*order—sequence*	la orden	*order—command*
el papa	*the pope*	la papa	*the potato*
el pez	*fish*	la pez	*pitch, tar*
el policía	*policeman*	la policía	*police force, policewoman*

See also ADJECTIVES, DEFINITE ARTICLES, and INDEFINITE ARTICLES.

NUESTRO(A): *See POSSESSIVE ADJECTIVES and POSSESSIVE PRONOUNS.*

NUMBER: *See NOUNS.*

NUMBERS: *See CARDINAL NUMBERS and ORDINAL NUMBERS.*

NUNCA: *See AFFIRMATIVE AND NEGATIVE INDEFINITES.*

O

O: *See OR: O VS. U. Also see AFFIRMATIVE AND NEGATIVE INDEFINITES.*

OBJECT PRONOUNS: *See DIRECT OBJECT PRONOUNS and INDIRECT OBJECT PRONOUNS.*

OÍR *(TO HEAR)*

Irregular Forms
Present Indicative: **oigo, oyes, oye, oímos, oís, oyen**
Preterit: **oí, oíste, oyó, oímos, oísteis, oyeron**
Present Subjunctive: **oiga, oigas, oiga, oigamos, oigáis, oigan**
Imperfect Subjunctive: **oyera,** etc.; **oyese,** etc.
Present Participle: **oyendo**
Past Participle: **oído**

OJALÁ

Ojalá means *I hope* or *I wish* and is followed by a verb in a subjunctive tense.

Ojalá (que) tengan la dirección.	***I hope*** *they have the address.*
Ojalá (que) no hayan vuelto.	***I hope*** *they haven't returned.*
Ojalá (que) no fuera con él.	***I wish*** *I weren't going with him.*
Ojalá (que) lo hubieran hecho.	***I wish*** *they had done it.*

OLD(ER)

Old for things is rendered by a form of **viejo.** For people, it is rendered by a form of **viejo** or **anciano.** *Older* is expressed by a form of **más viejo** for things and **mayor** for people.

Mis abuelos son **viejos (ancianos).**	*My grandparents are* **old.**
La estatua es **más vieja** que la fuente.	*The statue is* **older** *than the fountain.*
Mi tía es **mayor** que mi tío.	*My aunt is* **older** *than my uncle.*

OLER *(TO SMELL)*

Irregular Forms
Present Indicative: **huelo, hueles, huele,** olemos, oléis, **huelen**
Present Subjunctive: **huela, huelas, huela,** olamos, oláis, **huelan**
Imperative: **huele** (tú)

OR: O VS. U

In general, **o** translates *or,* but before a word beginning with **o-** or **ho-, u** is used instead. Between two numbers written as numerals, **ó** has an accent mark.

Óscar **o** Pablo	*Oscar* **or** *Pablo*
Pablo **u** Óscar	*Pablo* **or** *Oscar*
6 **ó** 7	*6* **or** *7*
seis **o** siete	*six* **or** *seven*
siete **u** ocho	*seven* **or** *eight*
minutos **u** horas	*minutes* **or** *hours*

See also AFFIRMATIVE AND NEGATIVE INDEFINITES and ACCENT MARK (HOMONYMS).

ORDINAL NUMBERS

Ordinal numbers are used less frequently in Spanish than in English.

primer(o)	*1st*	sexto	*6th*
segundo	*2nd*	séptimo	*7th*
tercer(o)	*3rd*	octavo	*8th*
cuarto	*4th*	noveno (nono)	*9th*
quinto	*5th*	décimo	*10th*

undécimo	*11th*	septuagésimo	*70th*
duodécimo	*12th*	octogésimo	*80th*
décimo tercio (tercero)	*13th*	nonagésimo	*90th*
décimo cuarto	*14th*	centésimo	*100th*
décimo quinto	*15th*	ducentésimo	*200th*
décimo sexto	*16th*	tricentésimo	*300th*
décimo séptimo	*17th*	cuadringentésimo	*400th*
décimo octavo	*18th*	quingentésimo	*500th*
décimo noveno (nono)	*19th*	sexcentésimo	*600th*
vigésimo	*20th*	septingentésimo	*700th*
vigésimo primero	*21st*	octingentésimo	*800th*
trigésimo	*30th*	noningentésimo	*900th*
cuadragésimo	*40th*	milésimo	*1,000th*
quincuagésimo	*50th*	dos milésimo	*2,000th*
sexagésimo	*60th*	millonésimo	*1,000,000th*

Ordinal numbers have masculine and feminine forms and agree in number and gender with the noun they modify. **Primero** and **tercero** shorten to **primer** and **tercer** when they precede masculine singular nouns. The feminine forms do not apocopate (have an abbreviated form).

el **primer** ejercicio	*the **first** exercise*
la **tercera** clase	*the **third** class*
el **tercer** episodio	*the **third** episode*

The compound forms of the ordinal numbers may be written as one word.

décimoquinto (décimo quinto)	*fifteenth*

After **décimo,** ordinal numbers are usually replaced by cardinal numbers.

el siglo **veinte**	*the **twentieth** century*
Carlos **quinto**	*Charles **the Fifth***
Luis **catorce**	*Louis **the Fourteenth***

Note that the definite article is not used to connect the name of a ruler, pope, and so on with the number that follows.

Ordinal numbers are often abbreviated in Spanish by adding the last letter of the number to the Arabic numeral, for example, 1° *(1st)* and 2ª *(2nd)*.

OS: *See DIRECT OBJECT PRONOUNS, INDIRECT OBJECT PRONOUNS, and REFLEXIVE PRONOUNS.*

OTRO(A)

Otro(a) means *other (one)* or *another (one)* and is not preceded by **un** or **una**.

No quiere esta pelota. Quiere **otra.**	*He doesn't want this ball. He wants **another one.***
Este remo no sirve. Deme **otro.**	*This oar isn't any good. Give me **another one.***
¿Te vas a comer los **otros** dulces? Sí, me voy a comer **los otros.**	*Are you going to eat the **other** candies? Yes, I'm going to eat the **others.***

P

P.M.

P.M. is translated as **de la tarde** *(afternoon)* or **de la noche** *(evening, night)*.

Empiezo a las dos **de la tarde** y termino a las diez **de la noche.**	*I begin at two P.M. and I finish at ten P.M.*

PARA: *See POR VS. PARA.*

PARTICIPLE: *See PAST PARTICIPLE, PRESENT PARTICIPLE, and GERUND.*

PASSIVE VOICE

A verb that indicates that the subject does not act, but is acted upon, is in the *passive voice*.

La ventana **fue abierta** por el niño.	*The window **was opened** by the child.*
Los tamales **serán hechos** por ella.	*The tamales **will be made** by her.*

Compare those sentences with these in the active voice:

El niño **abrió** la ventana.	*The child **opened** the window.*
Ella **hará** los tamales.	*She **will make** the tamales.*

In Spanish, the true passive voice is a combination of a form of **ser** plus a past participle, which agrees in number and gender with the subject. **Por** translates the English *by*. If *by* is not expressed, a reflexive construction with **se** generally replaces the true passive voice.

Los cadáveres **fueron descubiertos** el lunes **por** el policía.	*The bodies **were found** on Monday **by** the policeman.*
Se descubrieron los cadáveres el lunes.	*The bodies **were discovered** on Monday.*
La carta **será enviada por** el secretario mañana.	*The letter **will be sent by** the secretary tomorrow.*
Se enviará la carta mañana.	*The letter **will be sent** tomorrow.*
Se habla español aquí.	*Spanish **is spoken** here.*
Se venden condones en esta farmacia.*	*Condoms **are sold** in this pharmacy.*
Se vende alcohol en esta farmacia.*	*Alcohol **is sold** in this pharmacy.*

*The verb in the **se** construction (**se** + verb) usually precedes the subject with which it must agree in number.

See ACTIVE VOICE and SE.

PAST PARTICIPLE

The *past participle* of **-ar** verbs is formed by replacing the **-ar** of the infinitive with **-ado**. For **-er** and **-ir** verbs, the past participle is formed by dropping the **-er** or **-ir** and adding **-ido**.

habl**ar**	*to speak*	habl**ado**	*spoken*
com**er**	*to eat*	com**ido**	*eaten*
conduc**ir**	*to drive*	conduc**ido**	*driven*

If the stem of an **-er** or **-ir** verb ends in **a, e,** or **o,** an accent is placed over the **-í-** of the past participle ending.

c**a**er	*to fall*	caído	*fallen*
l**e**er	*to read*	leído	*read*
oír	*to hear*	oído	*heard*

Some common irregular past participles include the following:

abrir	*to open*	abierto	*opened*
cubrir	*to cover*	cubierto	*covered*
decir	*to say, tell*	dicho	*said, told*
escribir	*to write*	escrito	*written*
freír	*to fry*	frito	*fried*
hacer	*to do, make*	hecho	*done, made*
imprimir	*to print*	impreso	*printed*
ir	*to go*	ido	*gone*
morir	*to die*	muerto	*died/dead*
poner	*to put*	puesto	*put*
romper	*to break, tear*	roto	*broken, torn*
satisfacer	*to satisfy*	satisfecho	*satisfied*
ver	*to see*	visto	*seen*
volver	*to return*	vuelto	*returned*

When a verb is formed by adding a prefix to a verb that has an irregular past participle, the verb with the prefix usually has the same irregular features in the past participle as the original verb: **descubrir** *(to discover),* **descubierto** *(discovered);* **contradecir** *(to contradict),* **contradicho** *(contradicted);* **describir** *(to describe),* **descrito** *(described);* **deshacer** *(to undo),* **deshecho** *(undone);* **posponer** *(postpone),* **pospuesto** *(postponed);* **devolver** *(to return),* **devuelto** *(returned);* **envolver** *(to wrap),* **envuelto** *(wrapped);* and so on.

A past participle may be used with a form of **haber** to form a perfect tense, in which case it is a verb and invariable, that is, it always ends in **-o.** In all other cases (with a form of **estar** to show a resultant condition, with a form of **ser** to form the passive voice, as an adjective modifying the noun directly, etc.), the past participle functions as an adjective and agrees in number and gender with the noun it modifies (describes).

Ella no **ha llegado** todavía.	*She **hasn't arrived** yet.*
Ya **hemos comido.**	*We **have** already **eaten.***
La puerta **estaba cerrada** cuando llegué.	*The door **was closed** when I arrived.*
Las cuentas ya **están pagadas.**	*The bills **are** already **paid.***
Los paquetes **fueron envueltos** por el dependiente.	*The packages **were wrapped** by the clerk.*

Las drogas **fueron robadas** anoche.	*The drugs **were stolen** last night.*
Recojamos las tazas **rotas.**	*Let's pick up the **broken** cups.*
Me gusta la carne **asada.**	*I like **roasted** meat.*

PAST PERFECT TENSE INDICATIVE

The *past perfect tense indicative,* sometimes called the *pluperfect tense,* consists of the imperfect indicative tense of **haber** + a past participle. It usually translates **had** + a past participle. Pronoun objects must precede the auxiliary verb (**había, habías,** etc).

Yo no lo **había creído.**	*I hadn't believed it.*
Tú **habías comido** todo.	*You had eaten everything.*
Él (Ella, Ud.) ya se **había levantado.**	*He (She, You) had gotten up already.*
Nosotros te **habíamos gritado.**	*We had yelled at you.*
Vosotros **habíais ganado.**	*You had won.*
Ellos (Uds.) **habían mentido.**	*They (You) had lied.*

PAST PERFECT TENSE SUBJUNCTIVE

The *past perfect tense subjunctive* consists of the imperfect tense subjunctive of **haber** + a past participle. It may translate *had, would have,* or *might have* + a past participle. Pronoun objects must precede the auxiliary verb (**hubiera, hubieras,** etc). The past perfect tense subjunctive is used under essentially the same circumstances as the imperfect tense subjunctive. *See IMPERFECT TENSE SUBJUNCTIVE.*

Ella no creía que yo **hubiera regresado.**	*She didn't believe I **had (would have) returned.***
Mi papá tenía miedo de que tú te **hubieras perdido.**	*My father was afraid you **might have gotten lost.***
Ellos dudaban que él (ella, Ud.) **hubiera dicho** eso.	*They doubted that he (she, you) **would have said** that.*

Era improbable que nosotros lo **hubiéramos hallado.**	*It was improbable that we **would have found** it.*
Yo esperaba que vosotros no **hubierais salido.**	*I hoped you **hadn't left.***
Yo lo compré antes de que ellos (Uds.) lo **hubieran visto.**	*I bought it before they (you) **had seen** it.*
Si **hubiera llovido,** no habríamos jugado al golf.	*If it **had rained,** we would not have played golf.*

PAST TENSE: *See IMPERFECT TENSE INDICATIVE, PRETERIT TENSE, and PRETERIT VS. IMPERFECT.*

PEDIR *(TO ASK FOR)*

For conjugation, see *STEM-CHANGING VERBS: -IR. Also see ASK:* PEDIR *VS.* PREGUNTAR.

PENSAR *(TO THINK)*

For conjugation, see *STEM-CHANGING VERBS: -AR AND -ER.*
Pensar followed by **en** or **de** + an object means *to think about* or *think of* and when followed by an infinitive may translate as either *intend to* or *plan to.*

¡Ay querida! ¡Siempre **pienso en** ti!	*Oh darling! **I** always **think about** you.*
¿Qué **piensas de** Newt Gingrich?	*What **do you think of** Newt Gingrich?*
Pensaba darte una sorpresa.	***I intended to give** you a surprise.*
Pienso ir a nadar esta tarde.	***I plan to go** swimming this afternoon.*

PERFECT PROGRESSIVE TENSES: *See PRESENT PARTICIPLE.*

PERFECT TENSES

A *perfect tense* in Spanish is composed of a form of **haber** + a past participle. *See* HABER *and* PAST PARTICIPLES. *See also* CONDITIONAL PERFECT

TENSE, FUTURE PERFECT TENSE, PAST PERFECT TENSE INDICATIVE, PAST PERFECT TENSE SUBJUNCTIVE, PRESENT PERFECT TENSE INDICATIVE, and PRESENT PERFECT TENSE SUBJUNCTIVE.

PERHAPS: *See MAYBE.*

PERO: *See BUT:* PERO *VS.* SINO.

PERSON

In grammar, there are three *persons* in the singular (first person *[I]*, second person *[you]*, third person *[he, she, it]*), and three persons in the plural (first person *[we]*, second person *[you]*, and third person *[they]*). The verb form must agree with the person. In Spanish, formal *you* forms, **usted** and **ustedes,** require third-person singular and plural verb forms, respectively.

PERSONAL A: *See* A.

PERSONAL PRONOUNS

A *personal pronoun* is a pronoun that refers to a person: *he, she, I, me, him, us, them,* or in Spanish, **él, ella, yo, me, lo, nos, les,** and so on.

PLAY: JUGAR *VS.* TOCAR

For conjugations, see JUGAR and -CAR *VERBS.*
Jugar means *to play a game or sport* and is usually followed by **a** when the game or sport is mentioned. **Tocar** means *to play music or a musical instrument.*

De niño **jugaba a las damas.**	*As a boy, **I played checkers.***
¿Te gusta **jugar al tenis?**	*Do you like **to play tennis?***
Sabe **tocar la flauta.**	*She knows how **to play the flute.***

PLEASE

The most common expression of *please* is **por favor,** which is generally used with a verb in a command form. *See COMMANDS.* However, **favor de, tenga**

la bondad de, and **hágame el favor de** + infinitive are also formal expressions of *please*.

Hable más despacio, **por favor.**	*Please speak more slowly.*
Tenga la bondad de hablar más despacio.	*Please speak more slowly.*
Hágame el favor de hablar más despacio.	*Please speak more slowly.*
Favor de hablar más despacio.	*Please speak more slowly.*

PLUPERFECT TENSE(S): *See PAST PERFECT TENSE INDICATIVE and PAST PERFECT TENSE SUBJUNCTIVE.*

PLURALIZATION: *See NOUNS.*

POCO: *See LITTLE.*

PODER *(TO BE ABLE)*

Irregular Forms
Present Indicative: **puedo, puedes, puede,** podemos, podéis, **pueden**
Preterit: **pude, pudiste, pudo, pudimos, pudisteis, pudieron**
Future: **podré, podrás, podrá, podremos, podréis, podrán**
Conditional: **podría, podrías, podría, podríamos, podríais, podrían**
Present Subjunctive: **pueda, puedas, pueda,** podamos, podáis, **puedan**
Imperfect Subjunctive: **pudiera,** etc.; **pudiese,** etc.
Present Participle: **pudiendo**

In the present tense, **poder** usually translates *can* and, in the preterit or imperfect, *could.* The conditional tense of **poder** also translates *could,* but it refers to present or future actions. **Poder** is followed by an infinitive.

Puedo trabajar este sábado.	*I can work this Saturday.*
No **pudo** encontrar la solución.	*He couldn't (failed to) find the answer.*
Siempre **podíamos** contar con él.	*We could always count on him.*
Podría decirte mañana.	*I could (would be able to) tell you tomorrow.*

PONER *(TO PUT)*

Irregular Forms
Present Indicative: (yo) **pongo**
Preterit: **puse, pusiste, puso, pusimos, pusisteis, pusieron**
Future: **pondré, pondrás, pondrá, pondremos, pondréis, pondrán**
Conditional: **pondría, pondrías, pondría, pondríamos, pondríais, pondrían**
Present Subjunctive: **ponga, pongas, ponga, pongamos, pongáis, pongan**
Imperfect Subjunctive: **pusiera,** etc.; **pusiese,** etc.
Imperative: **pon**
Past Participle: **puesto**

Poner means *to put* or *to turn on,* and **ponerse** means *to put on (clothes), to become,* and *to begin.*

Ella **pone** los calcetines en el tocador.	*She **puts** the socks in the dresser.*
No **pongo** la televisión por la mañana.	*I don't **turn on** the television in the morning.*
Se **puso** nervioso.	*He **became** nervous.*
¿**Te pusiste** el collar?	*Did you **put on** your necklace?*
Después de la cena, voy a **ponerme** a estudiar.	*After supper, I'm going **to begin** to study.*

POR *VS.* PARA

Both **por** and **para** may translate *for,* but they are not interchangeable.

Uses of *por*

1. To express *in exchange for*

Pagué cinco pesos **por** los plátanos.	*I paid five pesos **for** the bananas.*

2. To express the motive, cause, or reason (*for the sake of, on behalf of, owing to,* etc.)

Lo hice **por** mi hija.	*I did it **for** my daughter.*

Lo hace **por** amor.	*He does it **out of** love.*
Abandonaron el poblado **por** el huracán.	*They abandoned the town **owing to** the hurricane.*

3. To express *by* with the agent in the passive voice

Fue terminado **por** el plomero.	*It was finished **by** the plumber.*

4. To express duration of time

Vivió en Saltillo **por** un año.	*He lived in Saltillo **for** a year.*

5. To express *for* before the object of an errand or mission, particularly after verbs of motion

Regresó **por** su cartera.	*He returned **for** his wallet.*
Fue al super **por** refrescos.	*He went to the supermarket **for** soft drinks.*

6. To express *per*

Manejaba a cien kilómetros **por** hora.	*He was driving a hundred kilometers **per** hour.*

7. To express *by means of*

Hablamos **por** teléfono.	*We talked **on** the phone.*
Voy **por** tren y regreso **por** avión.	*I'm going **by** train and returning **by** plane.*

8. To express *in the morning (afternoon, evening)*

Practico **por** la mañana, **por** la tarde y **por** la noche.	*I practice **in** the morning, **in** the afternoon, and **in** the evening.*

9. To express *through, along*

Caminaban **por** la playa.	*They were walking **along** the beach.*

10. To express inexact location

Él vive **por** allí.	He lives **around** there (**somewhere**).

11. With infinitives to express what remains to be done

Me quedan dos capítulos **por leer.**	I have two chapters left **to read.**

12. With **estar** to express to be in favor of

Yo estoy por hacerlo ahora mismo.	**I'm in favor of** doing it right now.

13. In certain idiomatic expressions

por algo	for some reason
por aquí	around here
por casualidad	by chance
¡Por Dios!	Good Lord!
por ejemplo	for example
por eso	therefore
por favor	please
por fin	finally
por lo contrario	on the contrary
por lo general	generally
por lo menos	at least
por lo tanto	therefore
por otra parte	on the other hand
por si acaso	in case
por suerte	fortunately
por supuesto	of course
por todas partes	everywhere

Uses of *para*

1. To express *in order to*

Se detuvieron **para** ver el paisaje.	They stopped **in order to** see the landscape.

2. To indicate *for* + destination or recipient

Las flores son **para** Alicia.	*The flowers are **for** Alicia.*
Salió **para** Barcelona.	*She left **for** Barcelona.*

3. To express *by (no later than)*

Llegaremos **para** el lunes.	*We will arrive **by** Monday.*

4. To express *for* indicating the intended purpose or use

Las cajas son **para** los libros.	*The boxes are **for** the books.*

5. To express *for* meaning *considering the fact*

Para niño, es muy fuerte.	***For** a child, he is very strong.*

6. When expressing a state or condition

Yo ya no sirvo **para** eso.	*I'm not any good **for** that anymore.*

7. With **estar** to express *to be about to*

Ya **están para** salir.	***They are about to** leave.*

In many statements either **por** or **para** may be used with a corresponding change in meaning.

Por ser niño, es muy activo.	*He is very active because he is a child.*
Para (ser) niño, es muy fuerte.	*He is very strong for a child.*
Todos estudiaron **por** el examen.	*Everyone studied because of the exam.*
Todos estudiaron **para** el examen.	*Everyone studied for the exam.*
Te voy a dar treinta dólares **por** el libro.	*I'm going to give you thirty dollars for (in exchange for) the book.*

Te voy a dar treinta dólares **para** el libro.	*I'm going to give you thirty dollars for (to be spent on) the book.*
Ellos están **por** salir.	*They are in favor of leaving.*
Ellos están **para** salir.	*They are about to leave.*

PORQUE *VS.* POR QUÉ: *See INTERROGATIVES.*

POSSESSION WITH DE

There is no apostrophe in Spanish, so a paraphrastic expression must replace the English apostrophe. This means that *Mary's purse* becomes *the purse of Mary* (**la bolsa de María**). Note the following examples.

el anillo de mi padre	*my father's ring (the ring of my father)*
el consultorio del médico	*the doctor's office (the office of the doctor)*
el horario de Raquel	*Raquel's schedule (the schedule of Raquel)*
¿De quién es la foto? Es de Beto.	*Whose photo is it? It's Beto's.*

See WHOSE: CUYO *VS.* ¿DE QUIÉN(ES)?

POSSESSIVE ADJECTIVES

Possessive adjectives have long and short forms in Spanish.

Short Forms

mi, mis	*my*
tu, tus	*your (familiar singular)*
su, sus	*his, her, their, its, your (formal)*
nuestro, nuestra, nuestros, nuestras	*our*
vuestro, vuestra, vuestros, vuestras	*your (familiar plural)*

Like other adjectives ending in **-o, nuestro** and **vuestro** have four forms and must agree in number and gender with the noun they modify. The other possessive adjectives have only two forms, singular and plural. Possessive adjectives agree with the thing possessed and not the possessor. Short-form possessive adjectives precede the noun they describe.

mi fracaso y **mis** éxitos	*my failure and **my** successes*
tu perro y **tus** gatos	*your dog and **your** cats*
nuestra abuela y **nuestro** abuelo	*our grandmother and **our** grandfather*
nuestras almas y **nuestros** cuerpos	*our souls and **our** bodies*
vuestra camioneta y **vuestro** coche	*your van and **your** car*
vuestras vacas y **vuestros** caballos	*your cows and **your** horses*
su papel y **sus** libros	*his **(her, your, their, its)** paper and his **(her, your, their, its)** books*

Because both **su** and **sus** *(his, her, your, their, its)* may be ambiguous, a paraphrastic phrase consisting of **de** + prepositional pronoun may replace them for clarification.

su contribución *or* la contribución **de él (ella, usted, ellos, ellas, ustedes)**	*his **(her, your, their, its)** contribution*
sus contribuciones *or* las contribuciones **de él (ella, usted, ellos, ellas, ustedes)**	*his **(her, your, their, its)** contributions*

Long Forms

mío, mía, míos, mías	*my, of mine*
tuyo, tuya, tuyos, tuyas	*your, of yours (familiar singular)*
suyo, suya, suyos, suyas	*his, her, their, its, your (formal), of his, of hers, etc.*
nuestro, nuestra, nuestros, nuestras	*our, of ours*
vuestro, vuestra, vuestros, vuestras	*your, of yours (familiar plural)*

The long-form possessive adjectives follow the noun they modify and must agree in number and gender with the thing possessed and not the possessor. In the case of a possible ambiguity with the form **suyo,** the previous paraphrastic forms (**de él, de ella,** etc.) may substitute for them as well. The long-form possessive adjectives may include the word *of* in their English translations, but **de** can't be used in the Spanish expressions.

¿Quieres probar unas recetas **mías?**	*Do you want to try some recipes of mine?*
Es problema **suyo.**	*It's a problem of his (hers, theirs, yours).*
Prefiero las ideas **tuyas.**	*I prefer your ideas.*
Laura me prestó unos discos **suyos.**	*Laura lent me some records of hers.*
Te voy a prestar una camisa **suya.**	*I'm going to lend you a shirt of his.*
Oyeron los gritos **nuestros.**	*They heard our shouts.*
Me cae bien el amigo **vuestro.**	*I like your friend.*

POSSESSIVE PRONOUNS

el mío, la mía, los míos, las mías	*mine*
el tuyo, la tuya, los tuyos, las tuyas	*yours (familiar singular)*
el suyo, la suya, los suyos, las suyas	*his, hers, its, theirs, yours (formal)*
el nuestro, la nuestra, los nuestros, las nuestras	*ours*
el vuestro, la vuestra, los vuestros, las vuestras	*yours (familiar plural)*

The possessive pronouns agree in gender and number with the noun they represent and have the same forms as the long-form possessive adjectives. Possessive pronouns are most often used with definite articles but may be used with indefinite articles and demonstrative adjectives as well. After forms of **ser,** the definite article is usually omitted but may be used for emphasis.

¿Trajiste tus maletas? Sí, traje **las mías.**	*Did you bring your suitcases? Yes, I brought **mine.***
Él no quiere a su tía pero nosotros queremos a **la nuestra.**	*He doesn't love his aunt, but we love **ours.***
Se curó mi herida pero no se curó **la suya.**	*My wound healed, but **his** didn't.*

Mis legumbres están cocidas; **las tuyas** están crudas.	*My vegetables are cooked; yours are raw.*
Esta basura no es **mía.** Es **vuestra.**	*This trash isn't mine. It's yours.*

Because **el suyo, la suya, los suyos,** and **las suyas** may be ambiguous, a definite article + **de** + a prepositional pronoun may substitute for clarification.

¿Vas a usar mi receta? No, voy a usar **la de él (ella, usted, ellos, ellas, ustedes).**	*Are you going to use my recipe? No, I'm going to use his (hers, yours, theirs, yours).*

PREFIXES

In general, Spanish and English prefixes are similar in form and meaning. **Des-, i-,** and **in-** often make a word mean its opposite, and **ir-** replaces **in-** when the first letter of a word is **r-.**

desaparecer	*to **dis**appear*
desarmar	*to **dis**arm*
inválido	*in**valid**
incapaz	*in**capable**
irregular	*ir**regular**
irresponsable	*ir**responsible**

The Spanish counterparts of English words that begin with an **s-** followed by a consonant begin with an **e-.**

espectador	*spectator*
estúpido	*stupid*
estampilla	*stamp*

PREGUNTAR: *See ASK:* PEDIR *VS.* PREGUNTAR.

PREPOSITIONAL PRONOUNS

mí	*me*	nosotros(as)	*us*
ti	*you (familiar singular)*	vosotros(as)	*you (familiar plural)*
él	*him, it*	ellos	*them*
ella	*her, it*	ellas	*them*
usted	*you (formal singular)*	ustedes	*you (formal plural)*

Prepositional pronouns are used as objects in prepositional phrases.

El boleto no es **para ti.** Es **para mí.**	*The ticket isn't **for you.** It's **for me.***
Pilar no quiso salir **sin él.**	*Pilar refused to leave **without him.***
¿Vienes **con nosotros?** No, voy **con ellos.**	*Are you coming **with us?** No, I'm going **with them.***
Hablan **de usted.**	*They are talking **about you.***
Entre tú y yo, se me hace difícil.*	***Between you and me,** it seems difficult to me.*
Bailó **contigo** y no **conmigo.**†	*She danced **with you** and not **with me.***

* The prepositions **entre** *(between)*, **incluso** *(including)*, and **según** *(according to)* are followed by the subject pronouns **yo** and **tú** instead of the prepositional pronouns **mí** and **ti.**

† **Contigo** *(with you)* and **conmigo** *(with me)* are special forms. *See REFLEXIVE PRONOUNS.*

PREPOSITIONS

Prepositions are invariable in form. They may be used with nouns, pronouns, infinitives, or adverbs to form prepositional phrases that function as adjectives or adverbs.

Es el coche **de Miguel.**	*It's **Miguel's** car.*
No quiere viajar **sin ella.**	*He doesn't want to travel **without her.***
Salieron **después de comer.**	*They left **after eating.***
Apaga las luces **antes de salir.**	*Turn off the lights **before leaving.***
Los necesito **para mañana.**	*I need them **for tomorrow.***

In Spanish, the infinitive, and not the present participle, follows a preposition.

Salió **sin decir** una palabra.	*He left **without saying** a word.*
Antes de cenar, voy a lavar el coche.	***Before eating** supper, I'm going to wash the car.*
Estoy cansado **de escuchar**te.	*I'm tired **of listening** to you.*

Common Spanish Prepositions

a	*to*
a causa de	*because of*
a pesar de	*in spite of*
a través de	*through*
acerca de	*about*
además de	*besides*
al lado de	*beside*
alrededor de	*around*
ante	*before*
antes de	*before*
bajo	*under*
cerca de	*near*
con	*with*
contra	*against*
de	*of, from*
debajo de	*under*
delante de	*in front of*
dentro de	*inside*
desde	*from, since*
después de	*after*
detrás de	*behind*
durante	*during*
en	*in, on, at*
encima de	*on top of, on*
en frente de	*in front of*
entre	*among, between*
frente a	*opposite, in front of*
fuera de	*outside of*
hacia	*toward*
hasta	*even, until*
junto a	*next to*
incluso	*including*
lejos de	*far from*
para	*for, to, toward, in order to, by*
por	*for, by, by means of, for the sake of, per*
salvo	*except*
según	*according to*
sin	*without*
sobre	*about, over*
tras	*after, behind*

Verbs with Prepositions

Many verbs require a preposition before any dependent noun, pronoun, or infinitive. Some verbs require a specific preposition before infinitives but may be followed by other prepositions in other constructions. The verb **ir,** for example, is followed by **a** before an infinitive but may be followed by many different prepositions depending on the specific situation.

Vamos **a** regresar el martes.	*We are going to return on Tuesday.*
Fueron **hasta** Oaxaca.	*They went **all the way to** Oaxaca.*
Ella va **para** la tienda.	*She is going **to** the store.*
Yo voy **por** el médico.	*I'll go **for** the doctor.*
Fuimos **de** México **a** Veracruz.	*We went **from** Mexico City **to** Veracruz.*
¿Vas **sin** ellos?	*Are you going **without** them?*

1. Verbs followed by **a**

Asistir *(to attend)* is usually followed by **a.**

Carlos asiste **a** la misa de las seis cada domingo.	*Carlos attends six o'clock mass every Sunday.*

For other common verbs usually followed by **a,** *see* **A.**

2. Verbs followed by **de**

Depender *(to depend)* is usually followed by **de.**

Todo depende **de** los precios.	*Everything depends **on** the prices.*

Other common verbs followed by **de** include

abusar de	*to abuse*
acabar de + inf.	*to have just* + past participle
acordarse de	*to remember*
alegrarse de	*to be happy about*
apartarse de	*to move away from*

aprovecharse de	*to take advantage of*
burlarse de	*to make fun of*
cambiar de	*to change (clothes, the subject, etc.)*
cansarse de	*to get tired of*
carecer de	*to lack*
compadecerse de	*to feel sorry for*
constar de	*to consist of*
cuidar de	*to take care of*
deber de	*must (in the sense of probability)*
dejar de	*to stop*
despedirse de	*to say goodbye to*
disfrutar de	*to enjoy*
enamorarse de	*to fall in love with*
enterarse de	*to find out about*
fiarse de	*to trust*
gozar de	*to enjoy*
haber de + inf.	*to be supposed to*
ocuparse de	*to attend (to a task)*
olvidarse de	*to forget*
preocuparse de	*to worry about*
quejarse de	*to complain about*
reírse de	*to laugh at*
servir de	*to serve as*
tratar de	*to try to*
tratarse de	*to deal with (be a matter of)*

3. Verbs followed by **con**

Casarse *(to get married)* is usually followed by **con.**

Él se casó **con** Adela.	*He married Adela.*

Other common verbs followed by **con** include

contar con	*to count on*
contentarse con	*to be satisfied with*
cumplir con	*to fulfill*
encontrarse con	*to meet (run into)*
meterse con	*to quarrel*
soñar con	*to dream about, of*
tropezar con	*to stumble on*

4. Verbs followed by **en**

Insistir *(to insist)* is usually followed by **en.**

Insistió **en** las servilletas azules.	*She insisted **on** the blue napkins.*

Other common verbs followed by **en** include

confiar en	*to trust*
consistir en	*to consist of*
convenir en	*to agree to*
entrar en	*to enter*
fijarse en	*to notice*
meterse en	*to get into*
pensar en	*to think about*
quedar en	*to agree on*
tardar en	*to delay in*

See INFINITIVE and VERBS + PREPOSITIONS + INFINITIVES.

PRESENT PARTICIPLE

The *present participle* of **-ar** verbs is formed by dropping the **-ar** from the infinitive and adding **-ando.** For **-er** and **-ir** verbs, the present participles are formed by dropping the **-er** or **-ir** and adding **-iendo.**

habl**ar**	*to speak*	habl**ando**	*speaking*
com**er**	*to eat*	com**iendo**	*eating*
escrib**ir**	*to write*	escrib**iendo**	*writing*

The present participle ending of **-er** and **-ir** verbs whose stem ends in a vowel is **-yendo.**

constru**ir**	*to build*	constru**yendo**	*building*
caer	*to fall*	ca**yendo**	*falling*
creer	*to believe*	cre**yendo**	*believing*

Stem-changing **-ir** verbs change **-o-** to **-u-** and **-e-** to **-i-** in the present participle.

medir	*to measure*	**midiendo**	*measuring*
morir	*to die*	**muriendo**	*dying*

See STEM-CHANGING VERBS: -IR.

The following common verbs have irregular present participles:

ir	*to go*	**yendo**	*going*
poder	*to be able to*	**pudiendo**	*being able*
decir	to say, tell	**diciendo**	*saying, telling*
podrir	to rot	**pudriendo**	*rotting*
venir	to come	**viniendo**	*coming*

In English, *by* frequently precedes the present participle, but in Spanish the present participle stands alone.

Practicando a diario, uno se mejora.	***By practicing*** *daily, you get better.*
Saliendo temprano, no nos verán.	***By leaving*** *early, they won't see us.*

See GERUND.

Progressive Tenses

Used with **estar,** the present participle forms the *progressive tenses,* which are a form of *to be* + a PRESENT PARTICIPLE in English.

Estoy leyendo.	***I'm reading.***
Estaremos pensando en ti.	***We will be thinking*** *about you.*
¿Estabas comiendo?	***Were you eating?***
Estuvo gastando mucho dinero.	***He was spending*** *a lot of money.*
Yo estaría viviendo en una cueva.	***I would be living*** *in a cave.*
He estado sudando toda la tarde.*	***I have been sweating*** *all afternoon.*
No creo que **haya estado viviendo** con ella.*	*I don't believe **he has been living** with her.*

*The perfect progressive tenses are a form of **haber** + **estado** + a present participle. *See* HABER.

Ir, andar, venir, seguir, and **continuar** are sometimes used instead of **estar** in progressive constructions to convey particular nuances of meaning.

Anda buscando las llaves.	*He is looking around for the keys.*
Viene buscando las llaves.	*He is looking for the keys (**moving toward speaker**).*
Va buscando las llaves.	*He is looking for the keys (**moving away from speaker**).*
Sigue buscando las llaves.	*He keeps on looking for the keys.*
Continúa buscando las llaves.	*He continues looking for the keys.*

PRESENT PERFECT TENSE INDICATIVE

The *present perfect tense indicative* is composed of the present indicative of the helping verb **haber** and a past participle. Direct object, indirect object, and reflexive pronouns precede the helping verb. The present perfect tense indicative translates *have* or *has* + a past participle.

Yo **he manejado.**	*I have driven.*
Tú te **has dormido.**	*You have fallen asleep.*
Él (Ella, Ud.) me **ha visto.**	*He (she, you) has seen me.*
Nosotros no lo **hemos roto.**	*We haven't broken it.*
¿Vosotros os **habéis desayunado?**	*Have you had breakfast?*
Ellos (Ellas, Uds.) **han regresado.**	*They (They, You) have returned.*

See HABER *and* PAST PARTICIPLES.

PRESENT PERFECT TENSE SUBJUNCTIVE

The *present perfect tense subjunctive* is composed of the present subjunctive of the helping verb **haber** and a past participle. Direct object, indirect object, and reflexive pronouns precede the helping verb. The present tense subjunctive may translate *have* or *has* + a past participle or *will have* or *may have* + past participle.

Andrés no cree que yo **haya ganado.**	*Andrés doesn't believe I have won.*
Ojalá que tú no me **hayas mentido.**	*I hope you haven't lied to me.*

Es posible que él lo **haya hecho.**	*It is possible he **may have done** it.*
Tienen miedo de que nosotros lo **hayamos encontrado** para entonces.	*They are afraid we **will have found** it by then.*
Dudo que vosotros **os hayáis sentado** con ellos.	*I doubt you **have sat down** with them.*
Me alegro de que ustedes (ellos, ellas) **hayan cambiado** de parecer.	*I am happy you (they) **have changed** your (their) minds.*

The present perfect tense subjunctive is used under similar circumstances and situations as the present tense subjunctive.

See HABER, *PAST PARTICIPLE and PRESENT TENSE SUBJUNCTIVE.*

PRESENT TENSE INDICATIVE

The present tense indicative of regular verbs is formed by dropping the **-ar, -er,** or **-ir** from the infinitive and adding the appropriate endings. *See INFINITIVES.* Subject pronouns, for example, **yo, tú, él,** and **ella,** are not required in Spanish. *See SUBJECT PRONOUNS.*

	HABLAR	COMER	VIVIR
	TO TALK	*TO EAT*	*TO LIVE*
yo	habl**o**	com**o**	viv**o**
tú	habl**as**	com**es**	viv**es**
él, ella, Ud.	habl**a**	com**e**	viv**e**
nosotros, nosotras	habl**amos**	com**emos**	viv**imos**
vosotros, vosotras	habl**áis**	com**éis**	viv**ís**
ellos, ellas, Uds.	habl**an**	com**en**	viv**en**

The present tense indicative has several possible translations. For example, in the affirmative **yo hablo** may translate *I speak, I do speak,* or *I am speaking,* and **él habla** may translate *he speaks, he is speaking,* or *he does speak.* In the negative, **yo no hablo** may translate as either *I don't speak* or *I am not speaking,* and **él no habla** may translate as either *he doesn't speak* or *he isn't speaking.* In the interrogative, **¿Habla usted?** may translate as either *Do you speak?* or *Are you speaking?* and **¿Habla él?** may translate either *Does he speak?* or *Is he speaking?* With adverbs of time, the present indicative may also translate as the future *will.*

Mis padres **trabajan** todos los días.	*My parents **work** every day.*
No **aprenden** mucho.	*They **aren't learning** a lot.*
¿**Vives** tú con tu novia?	*Do you **live** with your girlfriend?*
Mi mamá no **maneja.**	*My mother **doesn't drive.***
Nosotros **vivimos** en Flint.	*We **live** in Flint.*
Como más tarde.	*I will **eat** later.*
Yo te **hablo** mañana.	*I'll **talk** to you tomorrow.*

See INFINITIVES, NEGATION, and SUBJECT PRONOUNS.

PRESENT TENSE SUBJUNCTIVE

Forms

The *present tense subjunctive* of most verbs is formed by dropping the **-o** from the **yo** form of the present tense indicative *(see PRESENT TENSE INDICA-TIVE)* and adding the appropriate endings, for example, for **-ar** verbs, **-e, -es, -e,** etc., and for **-er** and **-ir** verbs, **-a, -as, -a,** etc.

	PREPARAR	ESCOGER	SALIR
	TO PREPARE	*TO CHOOSE*	*TO LEAVE*
Present Indicative:	(yo) prepar**o**	(yo) escoj**o**	(yo) salg**o**
que yo	prepar**e**	escoj**a**	salg**a**
que tú	prepar**es**	escoj**as**	salg**as**
que él, ella, Ud.	prepar**e**	escoj**a**	salg**a**
que nosotros(as)	prepar**emos**	escoj**amos**	salg**amos**
que vosotros(as)	prepar**éis**	escoj**áis**	salg**áis**
que ellos(as), Uds.	prepar**en**	escoj**an**	salg**an**

Verbs ending in **-car, -gar,** and **-zar** change **-c-** to **-qu-, -g-** to **-gu-,** and **-z-** to **-c-,** respectively, before adding the present subjunctive endings.

	SACAR	PAGAR	ABRAZAR
	TO TAKE OUT	*TO PAY*	*TO HUG*
que yo	sa**que**	pa**gue**	abra**ce**
que tú	sa**ques**	pa**gues**	abra**ces**

que él, ella, Ud.	saque	pague	abrace
que nosotros(as)	saquemos	paguemos	abracemos
que vosotros(as)	saquéis	paguéis	abracéis
que ellos(as), Uds.	saquen	paguen	abracen

Stem-changing **-ar** and **-er** verbs undergo the same stem changes as in the present indicative, for example, **-o-** to **-ue-** and **-e-** to **-ie-**. **Jugar** *(to play)* is the only verb that changes from **-u-** to **-ue-**. Stem-changing **-ar** and **-er** verbs do not change in the **nosotros** and **vosotros** forms of the present subjunctive.

	CONTAR *TO COUNT* o → ue	JUGAR *TO PLAY* u → ue	PERDER *TO LOSE* e → ie
que yo	cuente	juegue	pierda
que tú	cuentes	juegues	pierdas
que él, ella, Ud.	cuente	juegue	pierda
que nosotros(as)	contemos	juguemos	perdamos
que vosotros(as)	contéis	juguéis	perdáis
que ellos(as), Uds.	cuenten	jueguen	pierdan

See STEM-CHANGING VERBS: -AR AND -ER.
Stem-changing **-ir** verbs change **-o-** to **-u-** and **-e-** to **-i-** in the **nosotros** and **vosotros** stems. The other forms change the same way as in the present indicative, that is, **-o-** becomes **-ue-**, **-e-** becomes **-ie-**, and **-e-** becomes **-i-**.

	DORMIR *TO SLEEP* o → ue	PREFERIR *TO PREFER* e → ie	SERVIR *TO SERVE* e → i
que yo	duerma	prefiera	sirva
que tú	duermas	prefieras	sirvas
que él, ella, Ud.	duerma	prefiera	sirva
que nosotros(as)	durmamos	prefiramos	sirvamos
que vosotros(as)	durmáis	prefiráis	sirváis
que ellos(as), Uds.	duerman	prefieran	sirvan

See STEM-CHANGING VERBS: -IR.

The following verbs have irregular forms in the present subjunctive tense:

	IR *TO GO*	SER *TO BE*	DAR *TO GIVE*	ESTAR *TO BE*	SABER *TO KNOW*	HABER *TO HAVE*
yo	vaya	sea	dé	esté	sepa	haya
tú	vayas	seas	des	estés	sepas	hayas
él, ella, Ud	vaya	sea	dé	esté	sepa	haya
nosotros	vayamos	seamos	demos	estemos	sepamos	hayamos
vosotros	vayáis	seáis	deis	estéis	sepáis	hayáis
ellos(as), Uds.	vayan	sean	den	estén	sepan	hayan

Uses

The *subjunctive mood* is usually triggered by another expression or idea. Consequently, it occurs primarily in dependent clauses and generally conveys a certain subjectivity or uncertainty on the part of the speaker (or writer) regarding the assertion or action in question. The subjunctive is used to refer to things, conditions, or situations that are not yet accomplished facts or are not yet known to be real. The *indicative,* on the other hand, is used to describe things, conditions, or situations that are accomplished facts, habitual occurrences, or perceived to be real.

Note that the present subjunctive is normally used when the expression that triggers the subjunctive is a command or is in the present, present perfect, future, or future perfect tenses.

The present subjunctive is often translated as an infinitive or as the simple form of a verb in English.

Yo quiero que ella **cante.**	*I want her **to sing.***
Prefieren que ella **cante** hoy.	*They prefer (that) she **sing** today.*

The present subjunctive also has the following possible translations:

Yo dudo que ella **cante** aquí.	*I doubt she **sings** (is singing, **will** sing, **does sing, may sing**) here.*

The subjunctive is triggered by the following circumstances and conditions:

1. In noun clauses after verbs of volition, permission, or request, such as **aconsejar** *(to advise),* indirect object pronoun + **decir** *(to tell—when*

conveying an order), **desear** *(to want),* **exigir** *(to demand),* **insistir** *(to insist),* indirect object pronoun + **pedir** *(to request),* indirect object pronoun + **permitir** *(to permit),* **preferir** *(to prefer),* **querer** *(to want),* indirect object pronoun + **recomendar** *(to recommend),* and **sugerir** *(to suggest).*

Quiero que me **den** los informes.	*I **want** them to **give** me the information.*
Insisten en que nos **hospedemos** en el Hotel Hilton.	*They **insist** we **stay** at the Hilton Hotel.*
Me pide que **vuelva** pronto.	*He **asks** me to **return** soon.*

2. In noun clauses after verbs of emotion such as **alegrarse de** *(to be glad or happy),* **encantar** *(to really like or love),* **esperar** *(to hope),* **gustar** *(to like),* **sentir** *(to be sorry),* **sorprender** *(to be surprised),* **temer** *(to fear),* and **tener miedo de** *(to be afraid of)*

Yo **siento** que ella **esté** enferma.	*I **am sorry** she **is** sick.*
Ella **se alegra** de que **podamos** ir.	*She **is happy** we **can** go.*

3. In noun clauses after verbs of disbelief, uncertainty, or doubt such as **creer** *(to believe)* in a negative or interrogative sentence, **dudar** *(to doubt),* **no estar seguro** *(to be unsure),* and **negar** *(to deny)*

No creo que **sea** ella.	*I **don't believe** it **is** she.*
Dudan que les **pague** pronto.	*They **doubt** he **will pay** them soon.*
¿**Crees** tú que ellos **sepan** la verdad?	*Do you **think** they **know** the truth?*

Creer in an affirmative statement is usually followed by the indicative.

Sí, yo **creo** que ellos **saben** la verdad.	*Yes, I **believe** they **know** the truth.*

4. In noun clauses after impersonal expressions that convey volition, emotion, and doubt such as **es bueno** *(it is good),* **es importante** *(it is important),* **es mejor** *(it is better),* **es necesario** *(it is necessary),* **es preciso** *(it is necessary),* **es urgente** *(it is urgent),* **es horrible** *(it is horrible),* **es lástima** *(it is a shame or pity),* **¡qué lástima!** *(what a shame or pity!),* **es terrible** *(it is terrible),* **es difícil** *(it is unlikely),* **es dudoso** *(it is doubtful),* **es extraño** *(it is strange),* **es fácil** *(it is likely),* **es posible** *(it is possible),* **es probable** *(it*

is probable), **no es cierto** *(it is not true)*, **no es verdad** *(it is not true)*, and **puede ser** *(perhaps)*

Es necesario que tú **entiendas** todo.	*It is necessary for you to understand everything.*

Impersonal expressions that convey certainty, for example, **es verdad** *(it is true)*, **es cierto** *(it is certain)*, and **es obvio** *(it is obvious)* are followed by the indicative.

Es verdad que ella **tiene** mucho dinero.	*It is true that she has a lot of money.*

5. After **ojalá** *(I hope)*

Ojalá que **viva** cerca de mí.	*I hope she lives near me.*

6. After **tal vez, quizá** (or **quizás**), or **acaso** (all meaning *perhaps* or *maybe*) to emphasize uncertainty

Tal vez lo **puedan** hacer.	*Perhaps they can do it.*
Quizá(s) salgan el lunes.	*Maybe they will leave on Monday.*

When the uncertainty is not emphasized or the notion of future is stronger than that of uncertainty, these expressions are generally followed by the indicative.

Acaso él lo **sabe.**	*Perhaps he knows it.*
Tal vez vendrán mañana.	*Maybe they will come tomorrow.*

7. In adjective clauses after indefinite or nonexistent antecedents, whether found in declarative or interrogative sentences

¿Hay alguien que **sepa** la respuesta?	*Is there anyone who knows the answer?*
No hay nadie que **sepa** la respuesta.	*There isn't anyone who knows the answer.*
Busca **una pareja** que **baile** bien.	*He is looking for a partner who dances well.*

If the antecedent refers to specific persons or things, the indicative is used.

Hay dos estudiantes que **saben** la respuesta.	*There are two students who know the answer.*
Conoce a una muchacha que **baila** bien.	*He knows a girl who dances well.*

8. In adverbial clauses after **a fin (de) que** *(so that, in order that)*, **a menos que** *(unless)*, **antes (de) que** *(before)*, **con tal (de) que** *(provided that)*, **en caso (de) que** *(in case)*, **para que** *(so that, in order that)*, and **sin que** *(unless)*

Siempre juega al golf **a menos que llueva.**	*He always plays golf **unless it rains.***

9. In adverbial clauses after **aunque** *(although, even if)*, **como** *(like, as)*, **cuando** *(when)*, **después de que** *(after)*, **donde** *(where)*, **en cuanto** *(as soon as)*, **hasta que** *(until)*, **luego que** *(as soon as)*, **mientras** *(while)*, and **tan pronto como** *(as soon as)* when the information or action described is not a known or accomplished fact

Yo iré **aunque esté** lloviendo.	*I will go **even if it is** raining (in the future).*
Dice que me lo va a decir **en cuanto lo sepa.**	*He says he will let me know **as soon as he finds out.***

When the information or action described is not uncertain or is a known or accomplished fact, the indicative is used instead of the subjunctive after these expressions.

Voy a salir ahora **aunque está** lloviendo.	*I am going to leave now **even though it is** raining.*
Me lo dijo **en cuanto** lo **supo.**	*He told me **as soon as he found out.***

As prepositions, **antes de, después de, hasta, para, sin,** and the like are followed by the infinitive.

Salió **sin decir** nada.	*He left **without saying** anything.*
Leyó el periódico **después de cenar.**	*She read the newspaper **after eating supper.***

See PREPOSITIONS.

10. In **usted, ustedes, nosotros,** negative **tú,** and negative **vosotros** commands; *see COMMANDS (IMPERATIVES)*

See INDICATIVE MOOD VS. SUBJUNCTIVE MOOD, IMPERFECT TENSE SUBJUNCTIVE, PAST PERFECT TENSE SUBJUNCTIVE, and *PRESENT PERFECT TENSE SUBJUNCTIVE.*

PRETEND: FINGIR VS. PRETENDER

For conjugations of **fingir,** *see* -GER *AND* -GIR *VERBS.*
Fingir means *to pretend,* and **pretender** means *to seek.*

Finge estar dormida.	*She pretends to be asleep.*
No **pretenden** llegar a ricos.	*They don't seek to become rich.*

PRETERIT PERFECT TENSE

The *preterit perfect tense* is preceded by a conjunction of time. It is very uncommon in contemporary Spanish and has largely been replaced by the simple preterit tense.

The preterit perfect tense consists of the preterit tense of **haber** + a past participle and translates *had* + past participle. Pronoun objects precede the auxiliary verb.

yo	**hube**
tú	**hubiste**
él, ella, Ud.	**hubo** + past participle
nosotros(as)	**hubimos**
vosotros(as)	**hubisteis**
ellos(as), Uds.	**hubieron**

Ellos se fueron **en cuanto me hube dormido.**	*They left as soon as I had fallen asleep.*

PRETERIT TENSE

The *preterit tense* of regular verbs is formed by dropping the **-ar, -er,** or **-ir** from the infinitive and attaching the appropriate endings to the stem.

	GANAR *TO WIN*	**COSER** *TO SEW*	**ABRIR** *TO OPEN*
yo	gan**é**	cos**í**	abr**í**
tú	gan**aste**	cos**iste**	abr**iste**
él, ella, Ud.	gan**ó**	cos**ió**	abr**ió**
nosotros(as)	gan**amos**	cos**imos**	abr**imos**
vosotros(as)	gan**asteis**	cos**isteis**	abr**isteis**
ellos(as), Uds.	gan**aron**	cos**ieron**	abr**ieron**

The preterit translates as the simple past *(won, sewed, opened)* or as **did** + verb *(did sew, did win, did open)*. In a question, the preterit tense translates *did* and in the negative, *didn't*. The preterit is generally used for a single action that began and ended in the past.

Salió temprano.	***She left** early.*
¿**Se quejaron** del precio?	***Did they complain** about the price?*
No **compré** nada.	***I didn't buy** anything.*

See PRETERIT VS. IMPERFECT.

PRETERIT VS. IMPERFECT

The preterit and the imperfect indicative are both simple past tenses, but they cannot be used interchangeably. For forms, *see IMPERFECT TENSE INDICATIVE and PRETERIT TENSE.*

The preterit tense translates as a simple past tense or as *did* + verb (**trabajó,** *he worked* or *he did work;* **tomé,** *I drank* or *I did drink*). It is used in the following situations:

1. To relate single past actions

Mandé la carta ayer.	***I sent** the letter yesterday.*

2. To relate a series of past actions that occurred during a specific time frame in the past

Sí, **fui** a la playa quince veces el verano pasado.	*Yes, **I did go** to the beach fifteen times last summer.*

3. To indicate the beginning or the end of a past activity

El baile **comenzó** a las ocho y **terminó** a la una.	*The dance **began** at eight and **ended** at one.*

4. To indicate the length of time that something existed or occurred

Los dinosaurios **vivieron** en la tierra por más de sesenta millones de años.	*Dinosaurs **lived** on earth for more than sixty million years.*
Ella **fue** estudiante allí por cuatro años.	*She **was** a student there for four years.*

The imperfect tense indicative may also translate as a simple past tense or as *did* + verb provided that the reference is to a repeated or habitual action. It also translates as *used to* + verb, as *would* + verb when referring to the past, and as *was* or *were* + present participle. It is used in the following situations:

1. To describe repeated or habitual actions in the past

Ellos **jugaban** al básquetbol todas las tardes.	*They **used to play** basketball every afternoon.*
Me levantaba temprano todos los días.	*I **would get up** early every day.*

2. To describe an object, person, condition, or situation that one recalls from the past

Había muchos árboles en el parque.	*There **were** many trees in the park.*
Era una niña muy bonita e inteligente.	*She **was** a very pretty and intelligent little girl.*
Estaba muy cansado y **tenía** mucha hambre.	*I **was** very tired, and I **was** very hungry.*

3. To present an action in progress in the past

Ellas **lavaban** la ropa.	*They **were washing** the clothes.*
Mientras yo **trabajaba** ellos **jugaban.**	*While I **was working,** they **were playing.***

4. To tell time or age in the past

Eran las dos de la mañana.	*It **was** two in the morning.*
Yo **tenía** quince años entonces.	*I **was** fifteen years old then.*

5. To express mental states or attitudes (*wanted, knew,* etc.) in the past

El **quería** ser abogado.	*He **wanted** to be a lawyer.*
Yo no **sabía** que vivía allí.	*I **didn't know** he lived there.*
Nosotros ya los **conocíamos**.	*We already **knew** them.*

The preterit and imperfect tenses are often used together. In such cases, the imperfect generally describes the setting or tells what was going on while the preterit refers to the specific actions or occurrences that took place against that background.

Eran las tres de la tarde cuando yo **llegué.**	*It **was** three in the afternoon when I **arrived.***
Ella lo **vio** cuando **venía** a la escuela.	*She **saw** it when she **was coming** to school.*
Me puse el abrigo porque **llovía** y **hacía frío.**	*I **put on** my coat because **it was raining** and **it was cold.***
Nosotros **comíamos** cuando **ocurrió** la explosión.	*We **were eating** when the explosion **occurred.***
El **vivía** en San Antonio cuando la **conoció.**	*He **lived** in San Antonio when he **met** her.*

Because of the nature of the preterit and imperfect tenses, certain commonly used verbs change meaning depending on the tense.

	IMPERFECT	PRETERIT
querer	*wanted*	*tried, (negative) refused*
saber	*knew*	*found out*
conocer	*knew*	*met*
poder	*could (in one's mind)*	*managed to, (negative) failed*

Note the following examples:

Ella **quería** que la acompañaran pero ellos **no quisieron.**	*She **wanted** them to go with her, but they **refused.***
Él **quiso** abrir la ventana pero **no pudo.**	*He **tried** to open the window but he **couldn't (failed).***
Yo creo que lo **podía** hacer cuando era niño.	*I think I **could** do it when I was a child.*
Tú ya lo **sabías;** lo **supiste** la semana pasada.	*You already **knew** it; you **found out** last week.*
Ella ya lo **conocía;** lo **conoció** en Guadalajara.	*She already **knew** him; she **met** him in Guadalajara.*

PRIMERO: *See* BUEN(O).

PROGRESSIVE TENSES: *See PRESENT PARTICIPLE.*

PRONOUNS: *See DEMONSTRATIVE PRONOUNS, DIRECT OBJECT PRONOUNS, INDIRECT OBJECT PRONOUNS, POSSESSIVE PRONOUNS, PREPOSITIONAL PRONOUNS, REFLEXIVE PRONOUNS, RELATIVE PRONOUNS, and SUBJECT PRONOUNS.*

PRONUNCIATION: *See A NOTE ON PRONUNCIATION, ACCENT MARK, DIPHTHONGS, ELISION, and HIATUS.*

PUESTO

Past participle of **poner** *(to put).*

PUNCTUATION

Common Punctuation Marks

Sign	Spanish	English
	punto	*period*
	dos puntos	*colon*

Sign	Spanish	English
;	punto y coma	*semicolon*
,	coma	*comma*
. . .	puntos suspensivos	*suspension points*
—	raya	*dash*
-	guión	*hyphen*
( )	paréntesis	*parentheses*
[ ]	paréntesis cuadrados	*brackets*
{ }	corchetes	*braces*
« »	comillas	*quotation marks*
¿ ?	principio y fin de interrogación	*question marks*
¡ !	principio y fin de exclamación	*exclamation marks*
*	asterisco	*asterisk*
´	acento escrito (ortográfico)	*written accent*
¨	diéresis, crema	*dieresis*
~	tilde	*tilde*

Spanish and English punctuation are very similar; however, there are a few significant differences.

In addition to a question mark at the end of a question and an exclamation mark at the end of an exclamation, an inverted exclamation mark and an inverted question mark are used at the beginning of exclamatory and interrogative sentences, respectively. They are placed where the exclamation or question begins and thus may occur within the sentence.

Spanish uses a dash to indicate a change of speaker in dialogue. Quotation marks (« ») that are larger than English quotation marks and that are placed somewhat lower are generally used for citing what others have written.

Punctuation for numbers in Spanish is treated in a completely opposite fashion than in English. Spanish uses a comma where English uses a decimal point and uses a point where a comma is used in English. In Mexico, however, it is not uncommon to see numbers punctuated as they are in English.

Note the following examples:

—¿Vas a ir tú?	*"Are you going?"*
—Sí, yo voy a ir, ¿y tú?	*"Yes, I'm going; are you?"*
¡Dios mío! ¡Qué susto!	*My Lord! What a scare!*
Robaron $27.348,50 del banco.	*They stole $27,348.50 from the bank.*

See ACCENT MARK, DIERESIS, and TILDE.

QUÉ

Qué followed by a noun in an exclamation translates *What a.* . . . If the noun is modified, **tan** or **más** comes between the noun and the adjective. **Qué** followed by an adjective or an adverb in an exclamation translates *How.* . . .

¡**Qué** tesoro!	**What a** *treasure!*
¡**Qué** playa tan bonita!	**What a** *beautiful beach!*
¡**Qué** sueño más interesante!	**What an** *interesting dream!*
¡**Qué** aburrido!	**How** *boring!*
¡**Qué** necio!	**How** *foolish!*
¡**Qué** pronto!	**How** *quickly!*

When asking what color something is or what something is made of, **qué** is preceded by **de.**

¿**De qué** color son tus ojos?	**What** *color are your eyes?*
¿**De qué** es la ensalada?	**What** *is the salad* **made of**?

See also CUÁL *VS.* QUÉ, *INTERROGATIVES, and RELATIVE PRONOUNS.*

QUÉ *VS.* CUÁL: *See* CUÁL *VS.* QUÉ.

QUERER *(TO WANT, LOVE)*

Irregular Forms
Present Indicative: **quiero, quieres, quiere,** queremos, queréis, **quieren**
Preterit: **quise, quisiste, quiso, quisimos, quisisteis, quisieron**
Future: **querré, querrás, querrá, querremos, querréis, querrán**
Conditional: **querría, querrías, querría, querríamos, querríais, querrían**
Present Subjunctive: **quiera, quieras, quiera,** queramos, queráis, **quieran**
Imperfect Subjunctive: **quisiera, quisieras,** etc.; **quisiese, quisieses,** etc.

When translating *wanted,* it is usually best to use the imperfect indicative. The preterit may translate *tried to* in the affirmative and *refused to* in the negative. The imperfect subjunctive may translate *would like.*

Quería decirle.	*I wanted to tell her.*
Quise decirle.	*I tried to tell her.*
No quise decirle.	*I refused to tell her.*
Quisiera decirle.	*I would like to tell her.*

QUESTION MARKS: *See PUNCTUATION.*

QUESTION WORDS: *See INTERROGATIVES.*

QUESTIONS

Unlike English, Spanish does not require an auxiliary verb (*do, does, did, will,* etc.) to ask a question. A declarative sentence becomes a question in Spanish merely by inflecting the voice when speaking or by inserting question marks when writing. Subject pronouns are not required. When the subject is expressed in a question, it may precede the verb, but more often it follows the verb.

Mario salió temprano.	*Mario left early.*
¿Mario salió temprano?	*Did Mario leave early?*
¿Salió temprano Mario?	*Did Mario leave early?*
¿Salió Mario temprano?	*Did Mario leave early?*

Tú comes en restaurantes.	*You eat in restaurants.*
¿Comes tú en restaurantes?	*Do you eat in restaurants?*
¿Comes en restaurantes tú?	*Do you eat in restaurants?*
¿Comes en restaurantes?	*Do you eat in restaurants?*
¿Tú comes en restaurantes?	*Do you eat in restaurants?*

See INTERROGATIVES and PUNCTUATION.

QUIÉN(ES): *See INTERROGATIVES.*

R

RADICAL-CHANGING VERBS: *See STEM-CHANGING VERBS: -AR AND -ER and STEM-CHANGING VERBS: -IR.*

REALIZE: REALIZAR VS. DARSE CUENTA (DE)/ENTERARSE (DE)

For conjugations, *see* -ZAR VERBS *and* DAR. *To realize* meaning *to understand* or *to become aware of* is **darse cuenta (de)** or **enterarse (de).** *To realize* in the sense of *to fulfill* or *to attain* is **realizar.**

Por fin **se dio cuenta (se enteró)** de que ya no lo quería.	*He finally **realized** she no longer loved him.*
¿Cuándo **te** vas a **dar cuenta de** que las computadoras son necesarias?	*When are you going **to realize** that computers are necessary?*
Nunca voy a **realizar** mis sueños.	*I am never going to **realize** (**fulfill**) my dreams.*

REFLEXIVE PRONOUNS

me	*myself*	nos	*ourselves*
te	*yourself*	os	*yourselves*
se	*herself, himself, itself, themselves, yourself, yourselves*		

When reflexive pronouns are used with verbs that are generally used reflexively (**acostarse** *to go to bed,* **quejarse** *to complain,* **vestirse** *to get dressed,* etc.), the reflexive pronoun is usually not translated into English. However, when reflexive pronouns are used with verbs that are generally not used reflexively (**golpear** *to hit,* **oír** *to hear,* **ver** *to see,* etc.), they are translated into English and may translate *each other* instead of their usual translations. Reflexive pronouns are placed in relation to the verb according to the same rules as direct and indirect object pronouns.

See DIRECT OBJECT PRONOUNS and INDIRECT OBJECT PRONOUNS.

Yo nunca **me** quejo pero tú siempre **te** quejas.	*I never complain, but you always complain.*
Nos acostamos temprano.	*We go to bed early.*
¿No **se** vistieron?	*Didn't they get dressed?*
Nosotros **nos** vemos todos los días.	*We see **each other** every day.*
El niño **se** vio en el espejo.	*The child saw **himself** in the mirror.*
Se estaban golpeando.	*They were hitting **themselves** (**each other**).*
Se oyeron pero no **se** hablaron.	*They heard **each other**, but they didn't speak to **each other**.*
¿Qué **te** compraste? **Me** compré una cartera.	*What did you buy **yourself**? I bought **myself** a wallet.*

See REFLEXIVE VERBS.

After prepositions, the prepositional pronouns **mí, ti, nosotros,** and **vosotros** may be used reflexively. However, the prepositional pronouns **él, ella, ellas, ellos, usted,** and **ustedes** become **sí** when used reflexively. *With herself, himself, themselves, yourself,* or *yourselves* is always **consigo** and never **con sí.** **Mismo(a)** may be used with prepositional pronouns when they are used reflexively. *See PREPOSITIONAL PRONOUNS.*

Lo voy a hacer **para mí (mismo).**	*I am going to do it **for myself.***
¿Pensaste **en ti?**	*Did you think **about yourself**?*
Trabajamos **para nosotros (mismos).**	*We work **for ourselves.***
Ella lo compró **para sí (misma).**	*She bought it **for herself.***
Juan Carlos tiene una opinión muy positiva **de sí (mismo).**	*Juan Carlos has a very positive opinion **of himself.***

| Intercambiaron algunas ideas **entre sí.** | *They exchanged some ideas **among themselves.*** |

| Ellos lo llevaron **consigo.** | *They took it **with them.*** |

REFLEXIVE VERBS

Most Spanish verbs can be used either reflexively or nonreflexively. When the subject and the direct or indirect object of the verb refer to the same person or thing, the verb is being used reflexively. However, most verbs tend to be either reflexive or nonreflexive. A *reflexive verb* is normally used with a reflexive pronoun to convey its usual meaning. *See REFLEXIVE PRONOUNS.* When introducing reflexive verbs, textbooks generally attach **se** to the infinitive to help identify the verb as reflexive (**sentarse** *to sit down,* **levantarse** *to get up,* **bañarse** *to take a bath,* etc.). Because reflexive pronouns are simply direct or indirect objects that reflect the subject, they follow the same rules of placement as direct and indirect object pronouns. *See DIRECT OBJECT PRONOUNS and INDIRECT OBJECT PRONOUNS.*

Present Tense Indicative of *bañarse* (to take a bath)

yo **me baño**	*I take a bath*
tú **te bañas**	*you take a bath*
él, ella, Ud. **se baña**	*he, she, you, it take(s) a bath*
nosotros **nos bañamos**	*we take a bath*
vosotros **os bañáis**	*you take a bath*
ellos(as), Uds. **se bañan**	*they, you take a bath*

Common Reflexive Verbs

acostarse	*to go to bed*
afeitarse	*to shave*
divertirse	*to have a good time*
ducharse	*to take a shower*
enamorarse	*to fall in love*
enojarse	*to get mad*
lavarse	*to wash*
levantarse	*to get up*
quitarse	*to take off*
sentarse	*to sit*
sentirse	*to feel*
vestirse	*to get dressed*

¿A qué hora **te levantaste?**	*What time **did you get up?***
Me levanté a las ocho.	*I got up at eight.*
Fidel **se afeitó** y **se duchó.**	*Fidel **shaved** and **took a shower.***
¿Quieres **sentarte** aquí?	*Do you want **to sit** here?*
No, **me** quiero **sentar** allí.	*No, I want **to sit** there.*
Nos quitamos la ropa y **nos acostamos.**	*We **took** our clothes **off** and **went to bed.***
Estoy **enojándome.**	*I'm **getting mad.***
No **te enojes.**	***Don't get mad.***
Vas a **enamorarte** de ella.	*You're going **to fall in love** with her.*
Vístete.	***Get dressed.***
No quiero **vestirme** todavía.	*I don't want **to get dressed** yet.*

When the subject of a reflexive verb does not act upon itself, it does not use a reflexive pronoun.

Olga **se levantó** y después **levantó** a los niños.	*Olga **got up** and then **she got** the kids **up.***
Se puso la chaqueta y luego **puso** las cajas en el garaje.	*She **put on** her jacket and then **she put** the boxes in the garage.*
Voy a **lavarme** las manos.	*I am going **to wash** my hands.*
Voy a **lavar** el coche.	*I am going **to wash** the car.*

Some verbs are used reflexively and nonreflexively with a corresponding change in meaning.

dormirse	*to fall asleep*	dormir	*to sleep*
irse	*to leave* or *go away*	ir	*to go*
ponerse	*to put on*	poner	*to put*

Me dormí en la clase porque sólo **dormí** dos horas anoche.	*I **fell asleep** in class because I only **slept** two hours last night.*

Ellos **se fueron** hace una hora.	*They **left** an hour ago.*
Fueron al parque.	*They **went** to the park.*

Some verbs may be used either reflexively or nonreflexively with no significant change in meaning, such as **desayunar/desayunarse** *(to eat breakfast),* **morir/morirse** *(to die),* and **olvidar/olvidarse de** *(to forget).*

Yo **me desayuno** temprano y ella **desayuna** tarde.	*I **have breakfast** early, and she **has breakfast** late.*

REGULAR VERBS

Regular verbs are those with conjugated forms that follow the normal conjugation pattern in the tense considered. For example, **barrer** *(to sweep)* and **llorar** *(to cry)* are regular verbs in the present tense indicative:

Barrer: barro, barres, barre, barremos, barréis, barren
Llorar: lloro, lloras, llora, lloramos, lloráis, lloran

See PRESENT TENSE INDICATIVE.

REÍR (TO LAUGH)

For conjugation, *see* -EÍR *VERBS.*
Reír is normally used reflexively, and **de,** not **en,** translates *at.*

¿**Te ríes de** mí?	*Are you **laughing at** me?*
No, **me río de** este loco.	*No, **I'm laughing at** this crazy guy.*

RELATIVE PRONOUNS

que	*that, which, who, whom*
quien, quienes	*who, whom*
el (la) cual, los (las) cuales	*which, who, whom*
el (la, los, las) que	*which, who, whom*
lo cual	*which, what, that which*
lo que	*which, what, that which*
cuyo, cuya, cuyos, cuyas	*whose*
donde	*where*

A *relative pronoun* is used to join the pronoun's antecedent with a related group of words or clause. Although English often omits the relative pronoun, Spanish requires that the relative pronoun be expressed.

Aquí tienes el número **que** necesitas.	*Here is the number (**that**) you need.*

Que is the most commonly used relative pronoun. It may refer to singular or plural persons or things and may translate *that, which, who,* or *whom.*

Yo tengo la foto **que** él trajo.	*I have the picture (**that**) he brought.*
Voy a preguntarle a la señora **que** vive en frente.	*I'm going to ask the lady **who** lives across the street.*
Es el joven **que** vimos ayer.	*He is the young man (**whom**) we saw yesterday.*

Que is generally used after the prepositions **a, con, de,** and **en** to refer to places or things. **Donde** also refers to places, and **quien** or **quienes** are used after these prepositions to refer to people.

El coche **en que** íbamos se descompuso.	*The car (**that**) we were riding in broke down.*
Es el equipo **con que** juega él.	*It is the team **with which** he plays.*
Busco el lugar **de donde** se mandó la tarjeta.	*I'm looking for the place **from where** the card was sent.*
El joven **con quien** fui al partido es mi sobrino.	*The young man **with whom** I went to the game is my nephew.*
Ella es la profesora **de quien** les hablaba.	*She is the teacher **about whom** I was talking to you.*

Quien and **quienes** refer only to people and often replace **que** in nonrestrictive clauses (those that are set off by commas and serve simply to provide additional information rather than to identify the person).

Mi tío, **quien** ha trabajado muchísimo toda su vida, acaba de ganar la lotería.	*My uncle, **who** has worked very hard all of his life, just won the lottery.*
El hombre **que** vive allí es mi tío.	*The man **who** lives there is my uncle.*

Quien(es) and **el (la, los, las) que** are used to mean *he who, the one who, those who,* and so on.

Quienes no estudian, no aprueban la clase.	*Those who don't study, don't pass the class.*
El que juega, paga.	*He who plays, pays.*

El/la cual, los/las cuales, or **el (la, los, las) que** are used instead of **que** and **quien(es)** after compound prepositions; after prepositions of more than one syllable; and after **sin, por,** and **tras** to refer to both people and objects. They may also replace **que** and **quienes** after other short prepositions. They agree in number and gender with the antecedent.

Ésa es la razón **por la cual** llegó tarde.	*That is the reason (**that**) he arrived late.*
Las cajas **dentro de las cuales (que)** encontré los papeles **que** te enseñé, estaban en el sótano.	*The boxes **in which** I found the papers (**that**) I showed you, were in the basement.*
El muchacho **en frente del cual** te sentaste es mi primo.	*The boy **in front of whom** you sat is my cousin.*

El cual, el que, and their feminine and plural forms are frequently used to avoid ambiguity when there are two or more antecedents of different gender.

La amiga de mi primo, **la cual (que)** va a venir a la fiesta, es muy simpática.	*My cousin's friend, **who** is coming to the party, is very nice.*
La amiga de mi primo, **el cual (que)** está en México ahora, es muy simpática.	*The friend of my cousin, **who** is in Mexico now, is very nice.*

Lo cual and **lo que** translate *which* when the antecedent is a statement, a situation, or an idea instead of a specific noun. **Lo que** also translates *what* when the antecedent is not expressed.

Él se puso a gritar, **lo cual (que)** me sorprendió mucho.	*He began to shout, **which** really surprised me.*

Yo no sé **lo que** van a hacer ahora.	*I don't know **what** they are going to do now.*

See THAN.

Cuyo (cuya, cuyos, cuyas) is a relative possessive adjective that means *whose,* and it may refer to a person or thing. It agrees in gender and number with the noun it modifies. In a question, **de quién** is used to express *whose* instead of **cuyo.**

Es el señor **cuyas** hijas conocimos ayer.	*He is the man **whose** daughters we met yesterday.*
Ese animal tan raro, **cuyos** espolones son venenosos, es ornitorrinco.	*That strange animal **whose** spurs are poisonous is a platypus.*
¿**De quién** es la cartera?	***Whose** wallet is it?*

See WHOSE: CUYO VS. ¿DE QUIÉN(ES)?

REMEMBER: ACORDARSE VS. RECORDAR

In general, these two verbs are interchangeable. However, **acordarse** is used with reflexive pronouns and requires the preposition **de** when followed by an object. **Recordar** may also mean *to remind.* For conjugations, *see STEM-CHANGING VERBS: -AR AND -ER.*

No **me acuerdo.** *or* No **recuerdo.**	*I don't remember.*
¿**Te acordaste?** *or* ¿**Recordaste?**	*Did you remember?*
No **se acuerda** de los detalles. *or* No **recuerda** los detalles.	*He doesn't remember the details.*
Me *recordó* que la cita era a las siete.	*She **reminded** me that the appointment was at seven o'clock.*

RETURN: VOLVER VS. DEVOLVER

For conjugations, *see STEM-CHANGING VERBS: -AR AND -ER* (their past participles are **vuelto** and **devuelto,** respectively). **Volver** is used as an intransitive verb meaning *to come back (return).* **Devolver** is used as a transitive verb meaning *to give back (return) something to someone* or *to some place.* **Regresar** may substitute for **volver** but not usually for **devolver.**

Pienso **volver (regresar)** a Bogotá en mayo. Mi hermano ya **volvió (regresó).**	*I plan **to return** to Bogotá in May. My brother already **returned.***
Me **devolvió** el dinero que le presté.	*He **returned** the money to me that I lent him.*
Tengo que **devolver** el libro a la biblioteca.	*I have **to return** the book to the library.*

REUNIR *(TO JOIN, COLLECT)*

Reunir has regular forms in all tenses except for its accent marks.

Irregular Forms
Present Indicative: **reúno, reúnes, reúne,** reunimos, reunís, **reúnen**
Present Subjunctive: **reúna, reúnas, reúna,** reunamos, reunáis, **reúnan**
Imperative: **reúne**

ROTO

Past participle of **romper** *(to break, to tear).*

S

SABER *(TO KNOW)*

Irregular Forms
Present Indicative: (yo) **sé**
Preterit: **supe, supiste, supo, supimos, supisteis, supieron**
Future: **sabré, sabrás, sabrá, sabremos, sabréis, sabrán**
Conditional: **sabría, sabrías, sabría, sabríamos, sabríais, sabrían**
Present Subjunctive: **sepa, sepas, sepa, sepamos, sepáis, sepan**
Imperfect Subjunctive: **supiera, supieras,** etc.; **supiese, supieses,** etc.

The preterit tense of **saber** frequently translates *found out.* When meaning *to know how to,* **saber** is followed by an infinitive, usually without the intervening word **como** *(how).*

Él lo **supo** ayer pero yo ya lo **sabía** desde la semana pasada.	*He found it out yesterday but I already knew it since last week.*
¿Por qué toma el autobús?	*Why does he take the bus?*
Porque no **sabe manejar.**	*Because he doesn't know how to drive.*

See KNOW: SABER VS. CONOCER.

SABER VS. CONOCER: *See KNOW: SABER VS. CONOCER.*

SALIR (DE) *(TO LEAVE, GO OUT)*

Irregular Forms
Present Indicative: (yo) **salgo**
Future: **saldré, saldrás, saldrá, saldremos, saldréis, saldrán**

Conditional: **saldría, saldrías, saldría, saldríamos, saldríais, saldrían**
Present Subjunctive: **salga, salgas, salga, salgamos, salgáis, salgan**
Imperative: **sal** (tú)

See LEAVE: SALIR *VS.* DEJAR.

SALIR *VS.* DEJAR: *See LEAVE:* SALIR *VS.* DEJAR.

SAN *(SAINT) VS.* SANTO(A) *(SAINT)*

San is used before all masculine names except **Tomás** and **Domingo. Santa** is used before all feminine nouns.

San Pedro y **San** Pablo	*Saint Peter and Saint Paul*
Santo Tomás y **Santa** Teresa	*Saint Thomas and Saint Teresa*

SAVE: AHORRAR *VS.* SALVAR

Ahorrar means *to save* in the sense of saving time or money, and **salvar** is *to save* someone or something from an impending misfortune.

La enfermera me **salvó** la vida.	*The nurse saved my life.*
Ahorro mis monedas en una alcancía.	*I save my coins in a piggy bank.*

SE

Se has several distinct uses.

Se may be used as a reflexive pronoun.

Ellos **se** levantan tarde y **se** acuestan temprano.	*They go to bed early and get up late.*
Juan **se** queja de todo.	*Juan complains about everything.*

See REFLEXIVE PRONOUNS and REFLEXIVE VERBS.

Se may be used in a reciprocal sense meaning *each other.*

Pepe y Olga **se** quieren mucho, pero no **se** ven a menudo.	*Pepe and Olga love each other, but they don't see each other often.*

See REFLEXIVE PRONOUNS.

Se may be used as a substitute for the passive voice.

Aquí **se habla** español.	*Spanish **is spoken** here.*
Se oyó un balazo.	*A shot **was heard.***
Se oyeron cinco balazos.	*Five shots **were heard.***

See PASSIVE VOICE.

Se may be used impersonally, in which case it may mean *people, you, they,* or *one.*

Hoy en día **se tiene** que trabajar mucho para sobrevivir.	*Nowadays **one** has to work hard to survive.*
Se puede encontrar ropa fina en ese almacén.	***You can** find good clothes at that department store.*
No **se fuma** tanto hoy en día.	***People** don't **smoke** as much nowadays.*
Se festeja mucho en el Brasil.	***They party** a lot in Brazil.*

See PASSIVE VOICE.

Se may also be used as an indirect object pronoun.

No tengo el dinero. **Se** lo presté a Rocío.	*I don't have the money. I lent it to Rocío.*
Sergio le compró un anillo a Elsa pero no **se** lo ha dado todavía.	*Sergio bought a ring for Elsa, but he hasn't given it **to her** yet.*

See INDIRECT OBJECT PRONOUNS.

SEASONS (OF THE YEAR)

el invierno	*winter*	el verano	*summer*
la primavera	*spring*	el otoño	*fall*

The seasons are not capitalized in Spanish. They are usually used with a definite article. After forms of **ser** or after the prepositions **de** and **en,** the articles are often omitted.

La primavera es mi estación favorita.	***Spring*** *is my favorite season.*
El básquetbol es un deporte de (del) **invierno.**	*Basketball is a **winter** sport.*
Hace mucho calor en (**el**) **verano.**	*It is very hot in **summer.***

SER *(TO BE)*

Irregular Forms
Present Indicative: **soy, eres, es, somos, sois, son**
Imperfect Indicative: **era, eras, era, éramos, erais, eran**
Preterit: **fui, fuiste, fue, fuimos, fuisteis, fueron**
Present Subjunctive: **sea, seas, sea, seamos, seáis, sean**
Imperfect Subjunctive: **fuera, fueras,** etc.; **fuese, fueses,** etc.
Imperative: **sé** (tú)

See SER *VS.* ESTAR.

SER *VS.* ESTAR

For conjugations, *see* SER *and* ESTAR.
Because both verbs translate *to be,* some confusion may arise. Specific circumstances and situations govern the proper use of each verb.

Uses of *estar*

1. To indicate location

Estamos en el consultorio.	***We are*** *in the doctor's office.*
Fenway Park **está** en Boston.	*Fenway Park **is** in Boston.*

2. To indicate a state or condition (usually temporary) of a person or thing, usually resulting from a change

¿**Estás** enfermo? No, **estoy aburrido.**	***Are you*** *sick? No, **I'm** bored.*
Estaban muy cansados.	***They were*** *very tired.*
El dictador **está** muerto.	*The dictator **is** dead.*

3. To form the progressive tenses *(see PRESENT PARTICIPLE)*

Los niños **están jugando** en el patio.	*The children **are playing** in the patio.*
Estaban caminando por el parque.	*They **were walking** in the park.*
Estaré comiendo a las ocho.	*I **will be eating** at eight.*

4. With adjectives to remark on a state or condition that merits a comment, is unexpected, causes surprise, or represents a change from the norm

¡**Está** grande tu casa!	*Your house **is** really big!*
Está demasiado caliente este café.	*This coffee **is** too hot.*
Mi primo era delgadito pero ahora **está** muy gordo.	*My cousin was very slender, but **he is** really fat now.*
¡Ay! ¡No me toques con ese hielo! ¡**Está** frío!	*Hey! Don't touch me with that ice! **It's** cold!*

Uses of *ser*

1. To identify the subject by linking it to a predicate noun or pronoun

Ella **es** ingeniera.	*She **is** an engineer.*
Ese animal **es** danta.	*That animal **is** a tapir.*

2. To indicate origin

¿De dónde **eres** tú?	*Where **are you** from?*
Soy de Sacramento.	*I **am** from Sacramento.*

3. To indicate what something is made of

La alfombra **es** de lana y las cortinas **son** de algodón.	*The carpet **is** made of wool, and the curtains **are** made of cotton.*

4. To indicate possession/ownership

Son mis guantes.	*They **are** my gloves.*

La mochila **es** de Miguel.	*It is Miguel's backpack.*
¿De quién **es** el estéreo?	*Whose stereo is it?*

5. To indicate destination or recipient with **para** *(for)*

¿**Para** quién **son** las flores?	*Who are the flowers for?*
Son para mi mamá.	*They are for my mother.*

6. To indicate the time of day or other time expressions

Es la una y media.	*It is one thirty.*
Eran las cinco de la mañana.	*It was five in the morning.*
Ya **es** tarde.	*It is already late.*

7. To form impersonal expressions

Es importante comer bien.	*It is important to eat well.*
Sería necesario quedarnos allí.	*It would be necessary for us to stay there.*

8. To form the passive voice

Ese poema **fue** escrito por Neruda.	*That poem was written by Neruda.*

See PASSIVE VOICE.

9. To indicate when or where something takes place

El concierto **es** a las ocho.	*The concert is at eight.*
La junta **es** en el auditorio.	*The meeting is in the auditorium.*

10. With adjectives to indicate qualities or characteristics that are considered relatively permanent, basic, inherent, innate, or intrinsic to the individual or object described

Es una casa muy grande.	*It is a very large house.*

Las fresas **son** rojas.	*Strawberries **are** red.*
Los hipopótamos **son** gordos.	*Hippopotamuses **are** fat.*
El hielo **es** frío.	*Ice **is** cold.*

Comparison of *ser* and *estar*

Many adjectives may be used with forms of either **ser** or **estar,** but their meaning differs depending on which verb is used even when the English translation remains the same. In general, **ser** tells what the subject is like, whereas **estar** indicates a change or a particular circumstance or situation. Note the following examples:

¿Cómo son tus padres?	*What **are** your parents **like?***
¿Cómo están tus padres?	*How **are** your parents?*
Es muy nervioso.	*He **is** very nervous (a nervous person).*
Está muy nervioso.	*He **is** very nervous (about something).*
Es muy pálida.	*She **is** very pale (because of her complexion).*
Está muy pálida.	*She **is** very pale (owing to something).*
Las manzanas Granny Smith **son** verdes.	*Granny Smith apples **are** green.*
¡Esta manzana **está** verde!	*This apple **is** green (not ripe)!*
Eres una mujer muy bonita.	*You **are** a very pretty woman.*
¡**Estás** muy bonita!	*You **look** very pretty!*
Es un profesor aburrido.	*He **is** a boring professor.*
El estudiante **está** aburrido.	*The student **is** bored.*

Es muy viva.	*She is very lively (energetic).*
¡Está viva!	*She is alive!*

Son listos.	*They are clever (astute).*
Están listos.	*They are ready.*

SHOULD: *See* DEBER (DE).

SÍ (MISMO): *See REFLEXIVE PRONOUNS.*

SI *CLAUSES*

Si *(if)* is followed by the present indicative tense and not the present subjunctive tense. In a contrary-to-fact situation, **si** is followed by the imperfect subjunctive or the pluperfect subjunctive. If a past situation is not contrary to fact, that is, is considered factual, a past tense indicative follows **si.**

Si **tengo** el dinero, voy a comprar un boleto.	*If **I have** the money, I am going to buy a ticket.*
Si **tuviera** el dinero, compraría un boleto.	*If **I had** the money, I would buy a ticket.*
Si **hubiera tenido** el dinero, habría comprado un boleto.	*If **I had had** the money, I would have bought a ticket.*
Si **tenía (tuve)** el dinero, era (fue) porque había trabajado toda la semana.	*If **I had** the money, it was because I had worked the whole week.*

SINCE

Desde *(since)* is used with a point in time, and **desde hace** *(since/for)* is used with a period of time. **Desde hace** is generally used with the present tense in Spanish and not the present perfect tense as is the case with *since* in English.

Juan trabaja aquí **desde junio.**	*John has worked here **since** June.*
Juan trabaja aquí **desde hace dos meses.**	*John has worked (has been working) here **for two months.***

As a conjunction, *since* is expressed by **puesto que.**

Puesto que es obvio que no sabe la respuesta, no vamos a preguntarle.	***Since** it is obvious he doesn't know the answer, we aren't going to ask him.*

SINO: *See BUT:* PERO *VS.* SINO.

SPEND: GASTAR *VS.* PASAR

To spend money is **gastar,** and *to spend time* is **pasar.**

Gasté más de 2.000 dólares en Acapulco.	*I **spent** more than 2,000 dollars in Acapulco.*
¿Dónde **pasaste** tus vacaciones? **Pasé** mis vacaciones en la costa.	*Where did you **spend** your vacation? I **spent** my vacation at the coast.*

STEM-CHANGING VERBS: -AR *AND* -ER

Stem-changing (radical-changing) -**ar** and -**er** verbs have stems that undergo predictable changes in the present indicative; the present subjunctive; and the **usted, ustedes,** and **tú** commands as follows:

1. The -**e**- in the next-to-last syllable of the infinitive (**pensar, entender**) becomes -**ie**- (**pienso, piensas,** etc.; **entiendo, entiendes,** etc.).
2. The -**o**- in the next-to-last syllable of the infinitive (**volver, contar**) becomes -**ue**- (**vuelvo, vuelves,** etc.; **cuento, cuentas,** etc.).
3. The -**u**- in the verb **jugar** becomes -**ue**- (**juego, juegas,** etc.).

These changes never occur in the **nosotros** or **vosotros** forms (**pensamos, volvemos, entendéis, contáis**). In general, stem-changing verbs are introduced and identified as such in textbooks with (**ue**) or (**ie**) after the infinitive, for example, **pensar (ie), cerrar (ie), volver (ue), encontrar (ue),** and so on.

-e- → *-ie-* Stem-Changing Verbs (*-ar* and *-er*)

PENSAR *(TO THINK)*
Irregular Forms
Present Indicative: pienso, piensas, piensa, pensamos, pensáis, piensan
Present Subjunctive: piense, pienses, piense, pensemos, penséis, piensen
Commands: piense (Ud.), piensa (tú), no pienses (tú)

Other common verbs following the model of **pensar** include **cerrar** *(to close)*, **comenzar** *(to begin)*, **despertar** *(to awaken)*, **empezar** *(to begin)*, **perder** *(to lose)*, **querer** *(to want)*, **recomendar** *(to recommend)*, and **sentarse** *(to sit)*.

-o- → *-ue-* Stem-Changing Verbs (*-ar* and *-er*)

VOLVER *(TO RETURN)*
Irregular Forms
Present Indicative: vuelvo, vuelves, vuelve, volvemos, volvéis, vuelven
Present Subjunctive: vuelva, vuelvas, vuelva, volvamos, volváis, vuelvan
Commands: vuelva (Ud.), vuelve (tú), no vuelvas (tú)

Other common verbs following the model of **volver** include **acordarse** *(to remember)*, **acostarse** *(to go to bed)*, **contar** *(to count)*, **doler** *(to hurt)*, **encontrar** *(to find)*, **mover** *(to move)*, **mostrar** *(to show)*, and **recordar** *(to remember)*.

    Jugar *(to play)* is the only verb that changes **-u-** to **-ue-**. *See* JUGAR.

STEM-CHANGING VERBS: -IR

Stem-changing (radical-changing) **-ir** verbs have stems that undergo predictable changes in the present indicative; the present subjunctive; the preterit; the imperfect subjunctive; the present participle; and **usted, ustedes,** and **tú** commands as follows:

1. *-e-* → *-ie-/-i-* Stem-Changing Verbs (*-ir*)

The **-e-** in the next-to-last syllable of the infinitive (**mentir, preferir**) becomes **-ie-** (**miento, mientes,** etc.; **prefiero, prefieres,** etc.) in all forms (except the first and second persons plural) of the present indicative and the present subjunctive; and in **usted, ustedes,** and **tú** commands.

The **-e-** in the next-to-last syllable of the infinitive (**mentir, preferir**) becomes **-i-** in the third persons singular and plural of the preterit, the first and second persons plural of the present subjunctive, all forms of the imperfect subjunctive, and the present participle.

MENTIR *(TO LIE)*

Irregular Forms

Present Indicative: miento, mientes, miente, mentimos, mentís, mienten
Preterit: mentí, mentiste, mintió, mentimos, mentisteis, mintieron
Present Subjunctive: mienta, mientas, mienta, mintamos, mintáis, mientan
Imperfect Subjunctive: mintiera, mintieras, etc.; mintiese, mintieses, etc.
Commands: mienta (Ud.), miente (tú), no mientas (tú)
Present Participle: mintiendo

Other verbs following the model of **mentir** include **divertirse** *(to have a good time)*, **preferir** *(to prefer)*, **sentir** *(to feel)*, and **sugerir** *(to suggest)*.

2. *-e-* → *-i-* Stem-Changing Verbs (*-ir*)

The **-e-** in the next-to-last syllable of the infinitive (**pedir, repetir**) becomes **-i-** in all forms of the present indicative (except the first and second persons plural), all forms of the present subjunctive, the third persons singular and plural of the preterit, all forms of the imperfect subjunctive, and the present participle.

PEDIR *(TO ASK FOR)*

Irregular Forms

Present Indicative: pido, pides, pide, pedimos, pedís, piden
Preterit: pedí, pediste, pidió, pedimos, pedisteis, pidieron
Present Subjunctive: pida, pidas, pida, pidamos, pidáis, pidan
Imperfect Subjunctive: pidiera, pidieras, etc.; pidiese, pidieses, etc.
Commands: pida (Ud.), pide (tú), no pidas (tú)
Present Participle: pidiendo

Other common verbs that follow the model of **pedir** include **impedir** *(to impede)*, **medir** *(to measure)*, **repetir** *(to repeat)*, **servir** *(to serve)*, and **elegir** *(to elect)*.

3. *-o-* → *-ue-/-u-* Stem-Changing Verbs (*-ir*)

The **-o-** in the infinitive (**dormir**) becomes **-ue-** (**duermo, duermes,** etc.) in all forms (except the first and second persons plural) of the present indicative and the present subjunctive, and in **usted, ustedes,** and **tú** commands.

The **-o-** in the infinitive (**dormir**) becomes **-u-** in the third persons singular and plural of the preterit, the first and second persons plural of the present subjunctive, all forms of the imperfect subjunctive, and the present participle.

DORMIR *(TO SLEEP)*

Present Indicative: d**ue**rmo, d**ue**rmes, d**ue**rme, dormimos, dormís, d**ue**rmen
Preterit: dormí, dormiste, d**u**rmió, dormimos, dormisteis, d**u**rmieron
Present Subjunctive: d**ue**rma, d**ue**rmas, d**ue**rma, d**u**rmamos, d**u**rmaís, d**ue**r-man
Imperfect Subjunctive: d**u**rmiera, d**u**rmieras, etc.; d**u**rmiese, d**u**rmieses, etc.
Commands: d**ue**rma (Ud.), d**ue**rme (tú), no d**ue**rmas (tú)
Present Participle: d**u**rmiendo

Morir *(to die)* follows the model of **dormir.**

In general, **-ir** stem-changing verbs are introduced and identified in textbooks with **(ie, i), (ue, u),** or **(i, i)** after the infinitive: **mentir (ie, i), dormir (ue, u), pedir (i, i),** and so on.
See -EÍR *VERBS.*

STRESS

Stress refers to the vowel or syllable in a word which is pronounced with the greatest force or emphasis.
See ACCENT MARK.

STRONG VOWELS

The strong vowels are **a, e,** and **o.** *See DIPHTHONGS.*

SU(S): *See POSSESSIVE ADJECTIVES.*

SUBJECT PRONOUNS

yo *I* (first-person singular).

tú *you* (second-person singular, familiar). **Tú** is used when addressing a person with whom the speaker is on a first-name basis, such as a friend, a family member, or a pet. **Tú** may also be used in a contemptuous fashion. Therefore, when in doubt as to proper usage between **tú** and **usted,** it is better to side with the formal **usted.**

él *he* (third-person singular).

ella *she* (third-person singular).

usted *you* (second-person singular, formal). **Usted** may be abbreviated **Ud.** or **Vd.** and is used when addressing an adult stranger, a superior, an older person, and so on. **Usted** requires a third-person singular verb form.

nosotros(as) *we* (first-person plural). **Nosotros** is used when referring to an all-male or mixed group; **nosotras** is used when referring only to females.

vosotros(as) *you* (second-person plural, familiar). **Vosotros** is used almost exclusively in Spain and is the plural of **tú. Vosotros** is used when referring to an all-male group or mixed group; **vosotras** is used when referring only to females.

ustedes *you* (second-person plural, formal). **Ustedes** is the plural form of **usted** and of **tú** as well, outside of Spain. **Ustedes** is used when addressing more than one person and may be abbreviated **Uds.** or **Vds. Ustedes** requires a third-person plural verb form.

ellos(as) *they* (third-person plural). **Ellos** refers to two or more masculine nouns or to a combination of feminine and masculine nouns; **ellas** refers only to two or more feminine nouns.

Unlike English, Spanish does not require a subject pronoun with a verb when a noun is not used as the subject of the verb. Subject pronouns are optional in Spanish and, when used, may be placed either before or after the verb. Subject pronouns must agree with the proper form of the verb in each tense. In general, Spanish does not express the subject pronoun *it.*

Abro la puerta.	
Yo abro la puerta.	*I open the door.*
Abro yo la puerta.	
Abro la puerta **yo.**	

¿**Trabajaste** aquí?	
¿**Tú trabajaste** aquí?	*Did you work here?*
¿**Trabajaste tú** aquí?	
¿**Trabajaste** aquí **tú?**	

Está roto.	*It is broken.*

See CONJUGATE, ELLO, and PRESENT TENSE INDICATIVE.

SUBJUNCTIVE: *See PRESENT TENSE SUBJUNCTIVE, IMPERFECT TENSE SUBJUNCTIVE, PRESENT PERFECT TENSE SUBJUNCTIVE, and PAST PERFECT TENSE SUBJUNCTIVE.*

SUBJUNCTIVE (MOOD) VS. INDICATIVE (MOOD): *See INDICATIVE MOOD VS. SUBJUNCTIVE MOOD.*

SUFFIXES

Augmentative Suffixes (-*ón* and -*ote*)

The augmentative suffixes **-ón** and **-ote,** in addition to meaning *large,* may also convey a pejorative connotation. The corresponding feminine endings are **-ona** and **-ota.**

una soltera	*a single woman*
una solter**ona**	*an old maid*
un pájaro	*a bird*
un pajar**ote**	*a **large** bird*

-*azo*

The suffix **-azo** usually means *a blow with.*

Me dio un cabez**azo.**	*He gave me a head butt.*
Me di un martill**azo.**	*I hit myself with the hammer.*

Diminutive Suffixes

The diminutive endings **-cito(a)** and **-ito(a)** may not only suggest smallness in size but also convey a sense of affection.

el bebé	*the baby*	el beb**ito**	*the little baby*
mi mujer	*my wife*	mi mujer**cita**	*my dear wife*
una mentira	*a lie*	una mentir**ita**	*a little lie*

The diminutives are very commonly added to first names: **Fidel (Fidelito), Miguel (Miguelito), Juana (Juanita), Olga (Olguita), Paco (Paquito),** and so on. Note that words ending in **-go(a)** or **-co(a)** change to **-gui-** and **-qui-** respectively, before adding the diminutive endings.

Other common diminutive endings are **-illo(a), -cillo(a),** and **-ico(a).**

pájaro	*bird*	pajar**illo**	*little bird*
gorrión	*sparrow*	gorrion**cillo**	*little sparrow*
momento	*moment*	momen**tico**	*an instant*

-ería

The suffix **-ería** often indicates a place where something is made or sold.

Voy a la panad**ería** y despúes a la carnic**ería.**	*I'm going to the bakery and then to the meat market.*
Trabaja en una papel**ería.**	*She works at a stationery store.*

Pejorative Suffixes

The suffixes **-acho, -aco, -ote,** and **-ucho** often have derogatory meanings. They may be added to adjectives, nouns, and even a person's name to convey the speaker's scorn or contempt.

¡Yo le tengo miedo a ese perr**ote!**	*I'm afraid of that big old dog!*
Todos los ric**achos** son así.	*All rich people are like that.*
Ese Miguel**ucho** no hace nada.	*That Michael doesn't do anything.*

Corresponding Spanish and English Suffixes

Many Spanish and English cognates have corresponding suffixes.

Spanish	English
-dad: activi**dad**, autori**dad**	*-ty: activity, authority*
-tad: dificul**tad**, liber**tad**	*-ty: difficulty, liberty*
-ción: descrip**ción**, viola**ción**	*-tion: description, violation*
-ario: advers**ario**, diccion**ario**	*-ary: adversary, dictionary*
-ia: famil**ia**, histor**ia**	*-y: family, history*
-ia: compañ**ía**, sociolog**ía**	*-y: company, sociology*
-ista: art**ista**, dent**ista**	*-ist: artist, dentist*
-oso: fam**oso**, nervi**oso**	*-ous: famous, nervous*
-mente: clara**mente**, fácil**mente**	*-ly: clearly, easily*
-ecto: perf**ecto**, corr**ecto**	*-ect: perfect, correct*
-able: culp**able**, prob**able**	*-able: culpable, probable*
-ible: pos**ible**, terr**ible**	*-ible: possible, terrible*
-ente: difer**ente**, ag**ente**	*-ent: different, agent*
-ico: eléctr**ico**, públ**ico**	*-ic: electric, public*
-encia: evid**encia**, difer**encia**	*-ence: evidence, difference*
-ivo: posit**ivo**, atract**ivo**	*-ive: positive, attractive*
-ante: restaur**ante**, arrog**ante**	*-ant: restaurant, arrogant*
-tura: aven**tura**, tor**tura**	*-ture: adventure, torture*
-al: anim**al**, hospit**al**	*-al: animal, hospital*
-or: doct**or**, inspect**or**	*-or: doctor, inspector*
-ento: ac**ento**, cont**ento**	*-ent: accent, content*

Although the correspondence between Spanish and English is fairly reliable for the preceding suffixes, there are many exceptions that must be memorized, such as **realista** *(realistic)* and **temporal** *(temporary)* among others.
See VERY.

SUPERLATIVES

In English, the *superlative* form is usually either *-est (biggest, tallest, funniest)* or *most/least (most interesting, most exciting, least complicated,* etc.). In Spanish, the superlative is formed with a definite article (**el, la, los, las**) and **más** or **menos.** *In* is expressed by **de** after a superlative and not by **en.**

El béisbol es **el** deporte **más popular de** Puerto Rico.	*Baseball is **the most popular** sport in Puerto Rico.*
Cantinflas era **el** cómico **más chistoso de** México.	*Cantinflas was **the funniest** comedian in Mexico.*
Mi casa es **la más grande de** la vecindad.	*My house is **the largest one in** the neighborhood.*
La pulmonía es **la enfermedad menos común de** estas islas.	*Pneumonia is **the least common** disease in these islands.*

The following adjectives have irregular superlative forms:

bueno	*good*	el mejor	*the best*
malo	*bad*	el peor	*the worst*
viejo	*old*	el mayor	*the oldest (for people)*
joven	*young*	el menor	*the youngest*

Pelé era **el mejor** jugador **del** equipo.	*Pelé was **the best** player **on** the team.*
Esas revistas son **las peores de** todas.	*Those magazines are **the worst ones** of all.*
Yo soy **el mayor de** la familia.	*I am **the oldest in** the family.*
Mi hermana es **la menor.**	*My sister is **the youngest one.***

See COMPARATIVES and VERY.

SUYO (SUYA, SUYOS, SUYAS): *See POSSESSIVE ADJECTIVES and POSSESSIVE PRONOUNS.*

SYLLABIFICATION: *See DIPHTHONGS, DIVISION OF WORDS INTO SYLLABLES (SYLLABIFICATION), ELISION, and HIATUS.*

SYLLABLE: *See DIPHTHONGS, DIVISION OF WORDS INTO SYLLABLES (SYLLABIFICATION), and HIATUS.*

SYNTAX: *See WORD ORDER.*

T

TAKE: LLEVAR *VS.* TOMAR

Llevar means *to take* in the sense of *to carry or transport.* **Tomar** means *to take into one's possession* or *to take medicine, food, time, or a means of transportation.*

¿Me **llevas** al centro?	*Will you take me downtown?*
Tomó dos píldoras y se acostó.	*He took two pills and he went to bed.*
Tomaron el tren de París a Salzburgo.	*They took the train from Paris to Salzburg.*
Toma este dinero.	*Take this money.*

To take off is **quitarse,** and *to take out* is **sacar.**

Se quitó el saco.	*He took off his coat.*
Sacaron las cartas del cajón.	*They took the letters out of the drawer.*

TAL *(SUCH A)*

The indefinite articles (**un, una**) are not used after **tal.**

Tal mentira es una vergüenza.	*Such a lie is a disgrace.*
Tales cosas son el pan de cada día.	*Such things are very common.*

TAL VEZ: *See MAYBE.*

TAMPOCO: *See AFFIRMATIVE AND NEGATIVE INDEFINITES.*

TAN . . . COMO: *See AS . . . AS (TAN COMO).*

TANTO(A): *See AS (SO) MUCH/MANY AS (TANTO[S] . . .* COMO)

TE: *See DIRECT OBJECT PRONOUNS, INDIRECT OBJECT PRONOUNS, and REFLEXIVE PRONOUNS.*

TELEPHONE (NUMBER)

¿Cuál es su **número de teléfono**?	*What is your **telephone number?***
Mi número de teléfono es **2-35-45-50.**	*My telephone number is **235-4550.***

Note that after the initial single digit in an uneven combination, telephone numbers are recited in sets of two.

TELLING TIME: *See TIME OF DAY.*

TENER (TO HAVE)

Irregular Forms
Present Indicative: **tengo, tienes, tiene,** tenemos, tenéis, **tienen**
Preterit: **tuve, tuviste, tuvo, tuvimos, tuvisteis, tuvieron**
Future: **tendré, tendrás, tendrá, tendremos, tendréis, tendrán**
Conditional: **tendría, tendrías, tendría, tendríamos, tendríais, tendrían**
Present Subjunctive: **tenga, tengas, tenga, tengamos, tengáis, tengan**
Imperfect Subjunctive: **tuviera, tuvieras,** etc.; **tuviese, tuvieses,** etc.
Commands: **tenga** (Ud.), **ten** (tú), no **tengas** (tú)

Omission of Indefinite Articles after *tener*

Generally, the indefinite articles **(un, una, unos, unas)** are omitted after **tener** in negative sentences and in questions.

No tengo problema contigo.	*I don't have **a** problem with you.*
¿Tienes monedas?	*Do you have **any** coins?*

Tener in the preterit tense may mean *to get* or *to receive.*

Tuve una carta de ellos ayer.	*I **got** a letter from them yesterday.*

tener as *To Be*

Tener is used with certain nouns to express the English equivalent of *to be* + adjective. In these idiomatic expressions, **mucho** or **mucha,** not **muy,** translates *very.*

tener . . . años	*to be (so many) years old*
tener (mucho) calor	*to be (very) hot*
tener (muchos) celos	*to be (very) jealous*
tener (mucho) cuidado	*to be (very) careful*
tener la culpa	*to be to blame (at fault)*
tener (mucho) éxito	*to be (very) successful*
tener (mucho) frío	*to be (very) cold*
tener (mucha) hambre	*to be (very) hungry*
tener (mucho) miedo	*to be (very) afraid*
tener (mucha) prisa	*to be (in a big) hurry*
tener razón	*to be right*
no tener razón	*to be wrong*
tener (mucha) sed	*to be (very) thirsty*
tener (mucho) sueño	*to be (very) sleepy*
tener (mucha) suerte	*to be (very) lucky*
tener (mucha) vergüenza	*to be (very) ashamed*

¿Tienes hambre? No, pero **tengo mucha sed.**	*Are you hungry? No, but **I am very thirsty.***
Tendrá prisa.	***She must be in a hurry.***
Los niños no **tenían la culpa.**	*The children **were** not **to blame.***
¿Cuántos años tiene tu hermana? **Tiene veintidós años.**	***How old is** your sister? **She is twenty-two years old.***
Tiene muchos celos y no **tiene vergüenza.**	***He is very jealous,** and **he isn't ashamed.***

Other Idiomatic Expressions with *tener*

tener que ver con	*to have to do with*
tener presente	*to keep in mind*
tener catarro	*to have a cold*
tener derecho	*to have the right*
tener ganas de (+ infinitive)	*to feel like (doing something)*
tener en cuenta	*to have in mind*
tener lástima	*to feel sorry for*
tener la palabra	*to have the floor*

Eso no **tiene** nada **que ver con** su situación.	*That **has** nothing **to do with** his situation.*
Tengo catarro y me duele la cabeza.	*I **have a cold,** and my head hurts.*
¿Qué **tienes ganas de hacer**?	*What **do you feel like doing?***
Yo ya hablé. Usted **tiene la palabra.**	*I already spoke. You **have the floor.***

tener que + Infinitive

Forms of **tener que** + infinitive render versions of the English *have to, has to, had to,* or *must.*

¿Qué **tienes que hacer**?	*What **do you have to do**?*
Tengo que llenar el tanque.	*I **have to fill** the tank.*
Paco **tiene que revisar**lo todo.	*Paco **must check** everything.*
Tuve que decirle la verdad.	*I **had to tell** him the truth.*
Tendrá que terminarlo antes de las ocho.	*She **will have to finish** it before eight.*
Ojalá que no **tengamos que regresar** mañana.	*I hope **we don't have to return** tomorrow.*

See *HAVE:* TENER *VS.* HABER.

THAN

Than is usually translated by **que.**

Paco es más alto **que** su hermano mayor.	*Paco is taller **than** his older brother.*
Las niñas cantan con más entusiasmo **que** los niños.	*The girls sing more enthusiastically **than** the boys.*

Than is translated by **de** before a number and before a clause introduced by a relative pronoun.

Mi abuela tiene **más de quince** nietos.	*My grandmother has **more than** fifteen grandchildren.*

Than is translated by **de** before a clause. If the noun compared is the object of the verb in each clause, **del que, de la que, de los que,** or **de las que** is used, and the article agrees in number and gender with the antecedent. If the noun is not the object of both verbs or if an adjective or adverb is being compared, **de lo que** is used.

Él compró más comida **de la que** necesita.	*He bought more food **than (the food)** he needs*
Paco se come más tamales **de los que** vende.	*Paco eats more tamales **(than the tamales)** he sells.*
Él compró más comida **de lo que** yo creía.	*She has more money **than** I thought (she had).*
Es más fuerte **de lo que** parece.	*He is stronger **than** he looks.*
Pilar sabe más **de lo que** tú piensas.	*Pilar knows more **than** you think.*

Note that if the antecedent is a subject rather than an object, **que** is used to mean *than* instead of **de.**

Este examen tiene más preguntas difíciles **que** el que nos dio el profesor la vez pasada.	*This exam has more difficult questions **than** the one the professor gave us last time.*
Esas vacas están más gordas **que** las que vimos ayer.	*Those cows are fatter **than** the ones we saw yesterday.*

See COMPARATIVES and RELATIVE PRONOUNS.

THERE: AHÍ, ALLÁ, ALLÍ

Ahí translates *there* when referring to a place near the person addressed.

Allí translates *there* when referring to a location considered distant from the speaker.

Allá usually replaces **allí** with verbs of motion when referring to a location considered vague and far from the speaker.

Más allá translates *further on* or *beyond.*

¿Qué tienes tú **ahí**?	*What do you have **there**?*
Ellos se fueron al rancho ayer. Nosotros vamos a estar **allí** pasado mañana.	*They went to the ranch yesterday. We will be **there** the day after tomorrow.*
¡Mira! **Allá** van subiendo la cuesta de la montaña.	*Look! **There** they go up the slope of the mountain.*
Está **más allá** del parque.	*It is **beyond** the park.*

THERE + *TO BE*

English has many impersonal expressions with *there* + *to be* (*there is, there are,* etc.). In Spanish, these expressions are rendered by invariable forms of **haber.**

Indicative Forms of *haber* (there + to be)

hay	*there is, there are*
había	*there was, there were, there used to be*
hubo	*there was, there were*
habrá	*there will be*
habría	*there would be*
ha habido	*there has been, there have been*
había habido	*there had been*
habrá habido	*there will have been*
habría habido	*there would have been*

Ha habido muchos accidentes en esa carretera.	***There have been** many accidents on that highway.*
Había veinte estudiantes en la clase.	***There were** twenty students in the class.*
¿**Habrá** una fiesta mañana?	***Will there be** a party tomorrow?*

Subjunctive Forms of *haber* (there + to be)

haya   *there is, there are, there will be, there may be*

Ojalá que **haya** menos personas allí.   *I hope **there are** fewer people there.*

---

haya habido   *there has been, there have been, there will have been, there may have been*

No creo que **haya habido** mucha   *I don't believe **there has been** a lot of*
confusión.   *confusion.*

---

hubiera   *there was, there were, there used to be, there would be, there might be*

Tenía miedo de que **hubiera**   *He was afraid **there would be***
un desacuerdo.   *a disagreement.*

---

hubiera habido   *there had been, there would have been, there might have been*

Se alegraba de que no **hubiera**   *She was glad that **there had been***
habido más de una respuesta   *only one correct answer.*
correcta.

TI: *See PREPOSITIONAL PRONOUNS and REFLEXIVE PRONOUNS.*

TIEMPO: *See WEATHER EXPRESSIONS and TIME:*
HORA/RATO/TIEMPO/VEZ

TILDE

Tilde normally refers to the curlicue over **ñ**. Occasionally the term is used to refer to the written accent mark ´ (m**é**dico, bast**ó**n, etc).
See A NOTE ON PRONUNCIATION and ACCENT MARK.

TIME: HORA/RATO/TIEMPO/VEZ

The English word *time* has several translations in Spanish. **Tiempo** is used for **time** in a general sense and when referring to duration of time. *Time* in the sense of *occasion* is **vez,** and *time of day* is **hora.** A short *time (while)* is **un rato.**

No tengo mucho **tiempo** hoy.	*I don't have much **time** today.*
Te he dicho veinte **veces.**	*I have told you twenty **times.***
¿A qué **hora** te vas?	*What **time** are you leaving?*
Se quedaron **un rato.**	*They stayed **a while.***

TIME (OF DAY)

¿Qué hora es?	What time is it?

For all hours of the day except one o'clock, **son las** expresses *it is;* for one o'clock, *it is* is expressed by **es la.** There is no comparable Spanish expression for the English *o'clock.* Minutes after the hour are preceded by **y,** and minutes before the hour by **menos. Cuarto** *(quarter)* may substitute for **quince,** and **media** *(half past)* usually replaces **treinta.** A.M. is **de la mañana,** and P.M. is either **de la tarde** or **de la noche.** To tell time in the past, **eran las** *(it was)* is used for all hours except one o'clock, in which case **era la** *(it was)* is used.

Son las tres.	*It is three o'clock.*
Es la una.	*It is one o'clock.*
Son las cinco y diez.	*It is five ten.*
Era la una menos cuarto.	*It was a quarter to one.*
Son las once y media.	*It is eleven thirty.*
Son las cuatro de la tarde.	*It is four P.M.*
Eran las dos y cuarto de la mañana.	*It was two fifteen A.M.*

When asking what time something occurs or what time someone does something, the phrase **¿A qué hora . . . ?** *(What time . . . ?)* is used. **A las** *(at)* is used for all hours except one o'clock, in which case **a la una** *(at one o'clock)* is used. *Midnight* is **la medianoche,** and *noon* is **el mediodía.**

¿**A qué hora** comenzaste? **A las dos y cuarto.**	*What time did you begin?* *At two fifteen.*
¿**A qué hora** abren? **A la una y media.**	*What time do you open?* *At one thirty.*
Era **la medianoche.**	*It was **midnight**.*
Vamos **al mediodía.**	*We are going **at noon**.*

See TIME: HORA/RATO/TIEMPO/VEZ.

TITLES: *See DEFINITE ARTICLES.*

TOCAR: *See PLAY:* JUGAR *VS.* TOCAR.

TRAER *(TO BRING)*

Irregular Forms
Present Indicative: (yo) **traigo**
Preterit: **traje, trajiste, trajo, trajimos, trajisteis, trajeron**
Present Subjunctive: **traiga, traigas, traiga, traigamos, traigáis, traigan**
Imperfect Subjunctive: **trajera, trajeras,** etc.; **trajese, trajeses,** etc.
Commands: **traiga** (Ud.), **no traigas** (tú)
Present Participle: **trayendo**
Past Participle: **traído**

TRIPHTHONGS

A *triphthong* is a three-vowel combination consisting of a strong vowel (**a, e, o**) preceded by a weak vowel (**u** or **i**) and followed by **i** or **y.** The three vowels (or two vowels + **y**) in the triphthong are always in the same syllable: estud**iái**s, contin**uéi**s, Urug**uay,** and so on.
See DIPHTHONGS.

TU: *See POSSESSIVE ADJECTIVES.*

TÚ: *See SUBJECT PRONOUNS.*

TUYO(A): *See POSSESSIVE ADJECTIVES and POSSESSIVE PRONOUNS.*

U

U: *See OR: O VS. U.*

-UAR *VERBS*

Verbs ending in **-uar** are regular except for the use of the accent mark in certain forms.

CONTINUAR *(TO CONTINUE)*

Irregular Forms

Present Indicative: **continúo, continúas, continúa,** continuamos, continuáis, **continúan**

Present Subjunctive: **continúe, continúes, continúe,** continuemos, continuéis, **continúen**

Commands: **continúe** Ud., **continúen** Uds., **continúa** tú, **no continúes** tú

Other **-uar** verbs include **actuar** *(to act),* **evacuar** *(to evacuate), and* **situar** (to situate).

See -GUAR *VERBS.*

-UIR *VERBS*

Verbs ending in **-uir,** but not **-guir,** require a **-y-** in certain forms of several tenses.

DESTRUIR *(TO DESTROY)*

Irregular Forms

Present Indicative: **destruyo, destruyes, destruye,** destruimos, destruís, **destruyen**

Preterit: destruí, destruiste, **destruyó,** destruimos, destruisteis, **destruyeron**

Present Subjunctive: **destruya, destruyas, destruya, destruyamos, destruyáis, destruyan**

Imperfect Subjunctive: **destruyera, destruyeras,** etc.; **destruyese, detruyeses,** etc.

Commands: **destruya** Ud., **destruyan** Uds., **destruye** tú, no **destruyas** tú

Other common **-uir** verbs include **huir** *(to flee),* **construir** *(to construct),* **disminuir** *(to diminish),* **fluir** *(to flow),* and **instruir** *(to instruct).*

See -GUIR *VERBS.*

UN (UNO, UNA, UNOS, UNAS): *See INDEFINITE ARTICLES and CARDINAL NUMBERS.*

USTED(ES): *See PREPOSITIONAL PRONOUNS and SUBJECT PRONOUNS.*

V

VACACIONES *(VACATION)*

Vacaciones is always used in the plural in Spanish.

Tengo mis **vacaciones** en junio.	*I have my **vacation** in June.*

VALER *(TO BE WORTH)*

Present Indicative: (yo) **valgo**
Future: **valdré, valdrás, valdrá, valdremos, valdréis, valdrán**
Conditional: **valdría, valdrías, valdría, valdríamos, valdríais, valdrían**
Present Subjunctive **valga, valgas, valga, valgamos, valgáis, valgan**
Imperative: **val** or **vale** (tú)

valer la pena	*to be worthwhile*

—**No vale la pena,** corazón.	*"It's not worthwhile, dear."*

VER *(TO SEE)*

Irregular Forms
Present Indicative: (yo) **veo**
Preterit: **vi,** viste, **vio,** vimos, visteis, vieron
Imperfect Indicative: **veía, veías, veía, veíamos, veíais, veían**
Present Subjunctive: **vea, veas, vea, veamos, veáis, vean**
Imperfect Subjunctive: **viera, vieras,** etc.; **viese, vieses,** etc.
Past Participle: **visto**

VENIR *(TO COME)*

Irregular Forms
Present Indicative: **vengo, vienes, viene,** venimos, venís, **vienen**

Preterit: **vine, viniste, vino, vinimos, vinisteis, vinieron**
Future: **vendré, vendrás, vendrá, vendremos, vendréis, vendrán**
Conditional: **vendría, vendrías, vendría, vendríamos, vendríais, vendrían**
Present Subjunctive: **venga, vengas, venga, vengamos, vengáis, vengan**
Imperfect Subjunctive: **viniera, vinieras,** etc.; **viniese, vinieses,** etc.
Imperative: **ven** (tú)
Present Participle: **viniendo**

VERB TENSES: *See CONDITIONAL PERFECT TENSE, CONDITIONAL TENSE, FUTURE PERFECT TENSE, FUTURE TENSE, IMPERFECT TENSE INDICATIVE, IMPERFECT TENSE SUBJUNCTIVE, PAST PERFECT TENSE INDICATIVE, PAST PERFECT TENSE SUBJUNCTIVE, PRESENT PERFECT TENSE INDICATIVE, PRESENT PERFECT TENSE SUBJUNCTIVE, PRESENT TENSE INDICATIVE, PRESENT TENSE SUBJUNCTIVE, PRETERIT PERFECT TENSE, PRETERIT TENSE, and PRESENT PARTICIPLE.*

VERBS + INFINITIVES

When followed by an object or an infinitive, some verbs require an intervening preposition between the verb and the object or between the verb and the infinitive. For a discussion and listing of these verbs, *see PREPOSITIONS and* A. The following verbs do not require an intervening preposition when they are followed by an infinitive:

aconsejar	*to advise*
deber	*ought to, should*
dejar	*to let, allow*
desear	*to desire, want*
esperar	*to hope, expect*
mandar	*to order*
necesitar	*to need*
pensar	*to plan, intend*
permitir	*to permit*
poder	*to be able, can*
preferir	*to prefer*
prohibir	*to forbid, prohibit*
querer	*to want*
recomendar	*to recommend*

saber	*to know (how)*
sugerir	*to suggest*

Pensamos salir temprano.	*We **plan to leave** early.*
Prefiero ir solo.	*I **prefer to go** alone.*

¿VERDAD?

¿Verdad?, ¿no es verdad?, and ¿no? are Spanish "tag questions" and correspond to the English *does he?*, *did they?*, *isn't it?*, *will she?*, and so on. In general, ¿**no es verdad?** and ¿**no?** follow affirmative sentences, and ¿**verdad?** follows negative sentences. **Es verdad** *(It's true, that's right)* is not a tag question. Notice the punctuation.

Alfredo te dio el dinero, ¿**no?**	*Alfredo gave you the money, **didn't he?***
Me has dicho todo, ¿**no es verdad?**	*You have told me everything, **haven't you?***
Se parece a su hermana, ¿**no es verdad?**	*She looks like her sister, **doesn't she?***
No llovió anoche, ¿**verdad?**	*It didn't rain last night, **did it?***
No hay remedio, ¿**verdad?**	*There is no hope, **is there?***
Es verdad que los redactores saben su oficio.	*It **is true** that the editors know their job.*

VERY

Bien, muy, sumamente, and the suffix **-ísimo(a)** translate *very*. When adding **-ísimo** to an adjective or adverb ending in a vowel, the vowel is dropped before adding the suffix.

Estoy **sumamente** cansado.	*I am **very** tired.*
Llegó **muy** tarde.	*He arrived **very** late.*
El examen fue **bien** difícil.	*The exam was **very** difficult.*
Es un perro fe**ísimo.**	*It is a **very** ugly dog.*

VISTO

Past participle of the verb **ver** *(to see)*.

VOLVER *(TO RETURN)*

For conjugation, *see STEM-CHANGING VERBS: -AR AND -ER.*

Past participle: **vuelto**

volver a + infinitive	*to do something again*
Volvieron a salir.	*They went out again.*

volverse	*to become*
Se volvió loca después de esa desgracia.	*She became insane after that misfortune.*

See BECOME and RETURN: VOLVER VS. DEVOLVER.

VOS (VOSEO)

Vos, in certain areas of the Spanish-speaking world, is a substitute for **tú.** The verb forms that accompany **vos** are unique to these regions (**tú eres** → **vos sos, tú vienes** → **vos venís,** etc.). **Vos** is colloquial and is not considered standard Spanish.

VOSOTROS (AS): *See PREPOSITIONAL PRONOUNS and SUBJECT PRONOUNS.*

VOWELS

The strong vowels are **a, e, o,** and the weak vowels are **i,** and **u.**
    See A Note on Pronunciation (page 3), DIPHTHONGS, HIATUS, and TRIPHTHONGS.

VUELTO

Past participle of **volver** *(to return).*

VUESTRO (A): *See POSSESSIVE ADJECTIVES and POSSESSIVE PRONOUNS.*

WEAK VOWELS

The weak vowels are **u** and **i.** *See DIPHTHONGS, HIATUS, and TRIPH-THONGS.*

WEATHER EXPRESSIONS

Weather Expressions with *hacer*

In most weather expressions with **hacer, mucho,** not **muy,** translates *very.*

¿Qué tiempo hace hoy?	*What's the weather like today?* *How is the weather today?*
Hace (mucho) frío.	*It's (very) cold.*
Hace (mucho) calor.	*It's (very) hot.*
Hace (mucho) fresco.	*It's (very) cool.*
Hace (mucho) viento.	*It's (very) windy.*
Hace (mucho) sol.	*It's (very) sunny.*
Hace (muy) buen tiempo.	*It's (very) nice. The weather is (very) nice.*
Hace (muy) mal tiempo.	*It's (very) bad. The weather is (very) bad.*

Weather Expressions with *haber*

In weather expressions with **haber, mucho** or **mucha(s),** not **muy,** translates *very.*

Había (mucho) sol.	*It was (very) sunny.*

Hay (mucha) niebla (neblina).	*It is (very) foggy (misty).*
Hay (mucha) humedad.	*It is (very) humid.*
Hay luna.	*The moon is out.*
Hay nubes.	*It is cloudy.*

Weather Expressions with *estar*

Está (muy) nublado.	*It is (very) cloudy.*
Está despejado.	*It's clear.*
Está (muy) fresco.	*It is (very) cool.*

Llover means *to rain,* and **nevar** means *to snow.* For conjugations, *see STEM-CHANGING VERBS:* -AR *AND* -ER.

Llueve mucho aquí; **está lloviendo** ahora.	*It **rains** a lot here; **it's raining** now.*
Normalmente no **nieva** aquí en octubre pero anoche **nevó.**	*Normally it doesn't **snow** here in October, but it **snowed** last night.*

La nieve *the snow* and **la lluvia** *the rain* are nouns.

La nieve es blanca.	***Snow** is white.*
La lluvia cae principalmente en los llanos.	***The rain** falls mainly in the plains.*

WHERE: *See INTERROGATIVES.*

WHOSE: CUYO VS. DE QUIÉN (ES)

Whose as an interrogative is expressed by either **¿de quién?** or **¿de quiénes?**

Cuyo is *whose* as a possessive relative and never as an interrogative. **Cuyo (cuyos, cuya, cuyas)** agrees in number and gender with the thing possessed and not with the possessor.

¿**De quién** es el regalo?	***Whose** present is it?*
¿**De quién** son los dulces? Son de mi hermano.	***Whose** candies are they? They are my brother's.*
¿**De quiénes** son los dulces? Son de mis hermanos.	***Whose** candies are they? They are my brothers' and sisters'.*
El señor Díaz es el abogado **cuyos** hijos fueron arrestados anoche.	*Mr. Díaz is the lawyer **whose** sons were arrested last night.*
Quiero hablar con la mujer **cuyo** esposo ganó el premio.	*I want to speak with the woman **whose** husband won the prize.*

See RELATIVE PRONOUNS and INTERROGATIVES.

WILL: *See FUTURE TENSE.*

WONDER (I WONDER): *See FUTURE TENSE and CONDITIONAL TENSE.*

WORD ORDER

Spanish word order (syntax) differs from English syntax as follows:

1. A descriptive adjective usually follows the noun it modifies.

| Tiene un **perro negro** y una **gata blanca.** | *She has a **black dog** and a **white cat.*** |
| Necesitamos una **mesa redonda.** | *We need a **round table.*** |

2. The subject is commonly placed after the verb in questions, in exclamations, in subordinate clauses, in sentences beginning with an adverb, and after a quote in dialog.

¿**Cuándo trabajas tú?**	***When do you work?***
¡**Qué tonto soy yo!**	***How foolish I am!***
Voy a leer la novela **que me regaló mi esposa.**	*I am going to read the novel (**that**) **my wife gave me.***

Mañana llegará **Cecilia.**	*Cecilia will arrive **tomorrow.***
—¿Por qué no?—preguntó **él.**	*"Why not?" he asked.*

3. Object pronouns precede conjugated verb forms.

Le dije que **lo traería** el sábado.	*I told her I would bring it on Saturday.*
Ellos **nos lo dieron** ayer.	*They **gave it to us** yesterday.*

4. Some adverbs are very flexible in their placement and may be found before the verb, immediately after the verb, or at the end of the sentence.

Aquí se venden zapatos de buena calidad.	*Good quality shoes are sold **here.***
Se venden **aquí** zapatos de buena calidad.	*Good quality shoes are sold **here.***
Se venden zapatos de buena calidad **aquí.**	*Good quality shoes are sold **here.***

5. Spanish questions and declarative sentences never end in a preposition.

¿En qué estaba pensando?	*What was he thinking **about?***
¿Para qué lo quieres?	*What do you want it **for?***
Ella es la chica **con** quien él tuvo problemas.	*She is the girl he had problems **with.***

See ADJECTIVES, DIRECT OBJECT PRONOUNS, INDIRECT OBJECT PRONOUNS, and SUBJECT PRONOUNS.

WORD STRESS: *See ACCENT MARK and STRESS.*

WORSE/WORST: *See COMPARATIVES and SUPERLATIVES.*

WOULD: *See CONDITIONAL TENSE, IMPERFECT TENSE INDICATIVE, and IMPERFECT TENSE SUBJUNCTIVE.*

Y

Y: *See AND: Y VS. E.*

YO: *See SUBJECT PRONOUNS.*

YOU (TÚ, USTED, USTEDES, VOSOTROS): *See SUBJECT PRONOUNS.*

See also DIRECT OBJECT PRONOUNS, INDIRECT OBJECT PRONOUNS, PREPOSITIONAL PRONOUNS, and REFLEXIVE PRONOUNS.

YOUNG(ER)/YOUNG(EST): *See COMPARATIVES and SUPERLATIVES.*

Z

-ZAR VERBS

Verbs ending in **-zar** change the **-z-** to **-c-** in the **yo** form of the preterit tense, in all forms of the present subjunctive, and in **usted** and **ustedes** commands as well as in negative **tú** commands.

CRUZAR *(TO CROSS)*

Irregular Forms
Preterit: (yo) **crucé**
Present Subjunctive: **cruce, cruces, cruce, crucemos, crucéis, crucen**
Commands: **cruce** Ud., **crucen** Uds., **no cruces** tú

Other common **-zar** verbs include **abrazar** *(to hug),* **avanzar** *(to advance),* **bostezar** *(to yawn),* **comenzar** *(to begin),* **empezar** *(to begin),* **especializar** *(to specialize),* **lanzar** *(to throw),* and **reemplazar** *(to replace).*